THE ART OF BRITISH ROCK

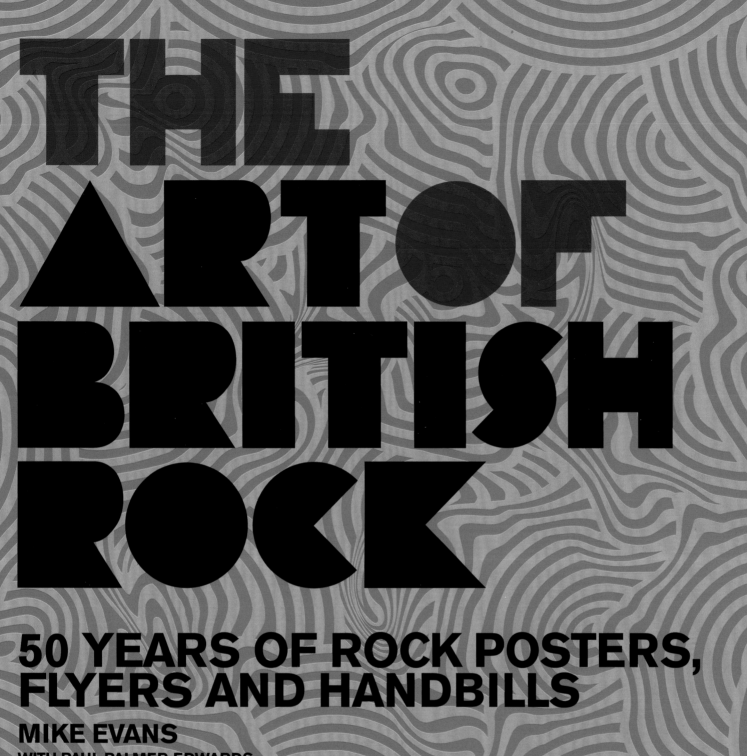

THE ART OF BRITISH ROCK

50 YEARS OF ROCK POSTERS, FLYERS AND HANDBILLS

MIKE EVANS

WITH PAUL PALMER-EDWARDS

F

FRANCES LINCOLN LIMITED

PUBLISHERS

Frances Lincoln Limited
www.franceslincoln.com

The Art of British Rock
Created by Elephant Book Company Limited, 35 Fournier Street, London E1 6QT
www.elephantbookcompany.com

Copyright © Elephant Book Company Limited 2010
First Frances Lincoln edition 2010; this paperback edition 2013.

Additional text by Ben Hubbard

Editorial Director: Will Steeds
Project Editor: Chris Stone
Editorial Consultant: Paul Palmer-Edwards
Editorial Manager: Laura Ward
Copyeditor: Ben Hubbard
Additional picture research: Clarissa Dolphin
Book and cover design: Paul Palmer-Edwards, Grade Design Consultants
Repro: Modern Age Repro House, Hong Kong

A catalogue record for this book is available from the British Library

ISBN: 978-0-7112-3473-4

Printed and bound in China

2 3 4 5 6 7 8 9

CONTENTS

FOREWORD
Artists on the art of British rock

'My designs are incredibly British in their look and nature. Working with the Who, it helps to be British to understand what they're all about.'
Richard Evans

'I wouldn't say that being British has purposely influenced the way I design apart from the fact that a designer would naturally assimilate visual information from the social environment he inhabits.'
John Pasche

'I have always approached life and work with a rather rebellious, if not downright contrary, attitude. And I tend towards favouring an eclectic palette, as that has always offered me the necessary freedom to manoeuvre, and to challenge. This has of course been identified as a typically British trait. But I do like to think my work has been influenced in equal measure by other, more obviously international, concerns.'
Malcolm Garrett

'My greatest inspiration are 1970s UK LP and single covers – growing up in the UK during this period, you were bombarded with such a variety of styles – techniques and crazy ass, out-on-a limb ideas, images – it just makes you go at the art thing with an 'anything goes' attitude.'
Chris Hopewell

'It's audio and it's visual. It's always been like that. You have the music and the art naturally follows.'
Richard Evans

'Any success I've had was born out of what happened musically here – the punk revolution and then the independent new wave record companies. That happened in Britain, so I don't think I could've done it anywhere else.'
Vaughan Oliver

'There will always be a need for graphic design. Rock 'n' roll is now all about brands, not bands.'
Richard Evans

'Music and the visual arts spring from the same source: the human imagination with natural phenomena as its foundation; the sounds and appearances of animals, air, water, fire and earth. All are expressions of the essential. There is a mystical correlation between color and sound. Every musical note is represented by a color, i.e. C–red, D–orange, E–yellow, F–green, G–blue, A–purple, B–violet, in the same progression as the rainbow. Human creativity is a historical "Fantasia" of music and art.'
Marijke Koger

'I think that strong visual presentations have developed from music genres because in many cases there are little or no restrictions placed on the designer. Inherent in the brief is often the encouragement to push the creative visual boundaries to the limit.'
John Pasche

'In every local music scene – from almost any era since 1966 – visual artists have been part of the scene. Local bands hire their friends from art school, to make their posters, handbills, badges, picture sleeves and adverts. It all springs from the same source. Music and the graphic arts complement, and in many ways, need each other.'
Dennis Loren

'Throughout most of the 20th century, music genres have been inextricably intertwined with the expression of personal style. Music and fashion like to go hand in hand, and cross-pollinate one another. Fashion initiates a sequence of visual events, where an expression of individuality has music as its rallying cry, and any accompanying visual presentation as its standard bearer.'
Malcolm Garrett

'No matter how strained their relationship may appear at times, it seems ridiculous to imagine a world where Sound and Vision would file for divorce.'
John Foross & Kjell Ekhorn, Non-Format Design

'Music is an abstract art in that any visual representation of the work is (usually) forced upon the music as part of its marketing, rather than as part of the performance of the music itself. At best, that visual layer is the result of a designer, image maker, artist or photographer who is able to amplify the experience of the music and place the sounds within an interesting and unusual visual context. At worst, the visual representation of music is the result of misguided interpretations of sales statistics and imitative, rather than innovative, thinking.'
John Foross & Kjell Ekhorn, Non-Format Design

'To be honest I have always seen myself as an artist, and our work as art – so the death of the record sleeve doesn't matter; also, I think it will evolve and metamorphose into some thing else anyway. I have recently been looking into the use of animated cover art for mp3 players and ipods. Artists have always adapted to and used new technology, so what difference does it make!'
Matt Carroll, Central Station

'When something's been designed well it's usually been designed by someone who is part of that culture, so they understand best the visual language which comes from the music.'
Vaughan Oliver

'Music has an irresistible attraction to visual artists – creating images for music is a bit like being one of the musicians or an arranger – it allows room for interpretation and objective presentation, and, strangely, has always been considered some kind of panacea for creative expression by young designers. This isn't always the case, but if you love music then it beats the pants off annual reports and biscuit tins.'
Rob O'Connor, Stylorouge

'The reason why the rock poster has had such a renaissance recently stems from the fact that people still want their music to have something tangible to it – downloads are great but people want to have and hold a piece of art that connects them to the band.'
Chris Hopewell

'The current digital download situation has certainly diminished the need for graphic design in terms of packaging but I believe that there will always be a strong union between music and imagery which will manifest itself in future digital formats.'
John Pasche

'There will always be a future for graphic design with respect to musical expressions. Musicians will still produce packaged CDs and have visual representations on their Myspace or Facebook pages. In addition, live performances demand promotion with visual back-ups such as flyers, posters, photos, stage projections and so on. Apart from talent, the "image" of a performer or band is of paramount importance.'
Marijke Koger

'Music packaging, in the formats we've been used to seeing for about 50 years or so, are fast disappearing, and rightly so. It wasn't that long ago that the only realistic chance anyone had to discover new music was to make a trip to a store where we'd be confronted by a multitude of 5" (or 12") square photos, illustrations and typographic compositions, whose sole purpose was to somehow substitute, visually, for the music they were applied to.

The experience of discovering new music has clearly changed beyond all recognition over the past decade, and for the better, but the technology available to connect the new music formats with any kind of visual representation has yet to fully mature.

The ubiquitous 240 pixel square digital "artwork" seems rather more like a pause for reflection before a period of renewed and fervent activity, than it seems a prediction of the total demise of album art.'
John Foross & Kjell Ekhorn, Non-Format Design

INTRODUCTION

Throughout its history, pop music has been promoted and celebrated through visual imagery. From the emergence of the genre as a powerful expression of a youthful counterculture in the late 1950s and 1960s, right up to the present day, the graphic art associated with it has in turn been influenced by a multitude of factors, not least of which has been an evolving print culture, and the technological developments that made such an evolution possible.

As important throughout, however, has been the wider cultural and economic – and demographic – context. Indeed, as rock music has developed over time, becoming more sophisticated and attracting larger and more diverse audiences, the images attached to the music have begun to define a more diverse cultural 'territory'.

Rock 'n' roll was born out of a generation rebelling against established values, and seeking to combine transgression and pleasure in new ways. The refusal to be defined by traditional family values created a heady environment of social and cultural experimentation amongst the young, which would express itself through protest, sex, drugs and rock 'n' roll, and would reach its zenith in the 'Swinging Sixties' scene in Britain.

This new young generation had more money to spend on leisure activities than any previous generation. Following a time of austerity after World War II, Britain – along with the US and Europe – experienced a long period of prosperity and economic growth, which would last until the early seventies. And in opposition to the stifling Victorian mores that many parents attempted to impose on their families, a new radical generational identity was being created, with its own voice, ideology and demands for social change. This new generation saw the British elite as amoral and painfully out of touch – an idea the elite did little to contradict. Instead, it would reveal its moral hypocrisy through several embarrassing political crises, notably Suez (1956) and the Profumo affair (1963).

But the opposing youth movement was no mere rabble. Many were learning about the deeper 'ideological' structure of society as a result of the 1960s expansion of higher education and its new social science subjects (usually considered 'Marxist' by the establishment). Higher education was further transformed through the ending of National Service in Britain in 1963, and a more equal gender balance. Suddenly the student community was bigger, younger, less deferential, and made up of boys and girls in relatively equal numbers. The university campus became the ideal environment for this population to meet, debate and socialize. The voice of youthful dissatisfaction was given a further platform through the explosion of new media in the sixties – television, magazines and, of course, popular music.

Not surprisingly then, things began to rock. For many, the sixties were fuelled by recreational drug use, sexual promiscuity and loud music – but also a new-found idealism. Young people felt sure that their new ideology and the sheer weight of their numbers would change the world.

The rock music giving a voice to these new views was initially promoted by means of material advertising gigs – concert and tour posters, and club flyers. The modern poster had first appeared a hundred years earlier, in the 1860s, with the invention of colour lithography. Lithography was slow and expensive; and yet even with the advent of faster methods of poster production in World War II (developed in response to the need for propaganda material), a single poster would require a large print run to justify the cost of making it up. Thus well into the 20th century, poster art was associated chiefly with the advertising of large organizations such as London Transport, Shell and the General Post Office, among others.

By comparison, the posters associated with popular music derived, in the first instance, from a parallel 'vernacular' tradition of printing, poster design and sign writing, and production of this early promotional material was similarly devolved locally. This tradition stemmed from 19th-century variety hall playbills, painted shop fronts and popular book jackets, and was generally separate from the evolution of graphic design.

These early posters would advertise 1960s 'beat boom' gigs, spearheaded by bands such as the Beatles. The beat boom, which would nurture the sixties rock revolution, had its roots in small jazz clubs rather than big concert venues, and as a result the posters promoting these gigs often broke away from the templates associated with larger concert halls (the old 'variety', or 'boxing match' style). Instead, local commercial artists – sometimes self-employed, sometimes employed by local printers – would create more off-the-cuff, improvised posters.

As the 1960s progressed, the influence of art school on popular culture and music would lead the rock artwork charge. Art school became a mixing pot, where cultural and musical ideas could forge a visual identity. The schools would also act as a testing ground for the new breakthrough processes of photo-mechanical screen-printing. Now typography, photography and illustration could be combined in ways never thought possible.

During the mid- to late-1960s, as the music became more psychedelic, there was an explosion of psychedelic poster art on both sides of the Atlantic. Illustrators and graphic designers now increasingly took the creative initiative. The development of Letraset opened up the options, making a huge number of typefaces and letterforms widely available for the first time. New fluorescent printing inks made everything brighter. As the counter-culture developed, the neatness of professional design associated with established cultural norms was abandoned for more fluid forms of design, clashing colours and eclectic types. Text was now closely integrated with photography and graphic images. In the early 1970s, photographically derived covers reached a peak of complexity and sophistication. Which would all be rejected again for the more visceral, home-made and 'thrown-together' approach of seventies punk. Every subsequent development would be based on punk's ideal of image assembly created by cutting and pasting. From the mid-nineties, the process would again change for the digital age, with computer screens taking centre stage for rock artwork design.

The history of rock music cannot be disentangled from the history of rock art. Every development in rock music – be it prog rock, punk, Brit pop or techno rock – has triggered an accompanying innovation in graphic style. Some of the key players to emerge from the graphic design world have become celebrities in their own right, and their work is instantly associated with a particular musical genre – for example, Roger Dean with prog rock, Jamie Reid with punk, Barney Bubbles with new wave, and Vaughan Oliver with post-punk alternative rock.

In putting together a book such as this, we have had to rely on a diversity of sources, from private collections to designers' own archives. The book would have proved impossible to compile were it not for the contribution of collectors, who have given us access to their 'vaults', along with individual designers and design studios, record companies and book publishers, who have allowed us into their archives.

What follows, however, isn't just a nostalgic look back at the history of rock music through the lens of its visual manifestation, but a celebration of British rock art as a vibrant creative medium that continues to flourish today. The sheer scope of styles and techniques in contemporary posters and album packaging is as great as the music it was created to promote. As the CD market and album sales decline, bands are once more relying on live touring as a major source of income. The consequent revival of the concert poster has meant a 21st-century renaissance in music-related illustration and design – and a new chapter in the six-decade history of the Art of British Rock, celebrated in the pages that follow.

Mike Evans

THE ROCK N ROLL ERA

POP GOES THE EASEL

The earliest examples of rock publicity design in Britain reflected the previous musical era which, in the mid-1950s, was being relegated to the history books by rock 'n' roll. Gig posters for pop shows in cinemas and civic halls were generally created by printers who, with their use of a limited range of (usually wooden) display fonts – used for the large letters – and a similarly restricted number of body text fonts, subscribed to the 'variety bill' promotional style of the venues in question.

When the first American rock stars, such as Bill Haley and Buddy Holly, toured Britain, it was as part of multi-act 'package' shows. These usually featured a mixed bag of British support acts in the good-old variety tradition – ballad singers, comedians and the like – rather than artists appealing specifically to a 'teen' pop audience. Tours by home-grown rockers – Cliff Richard and Billy Fury were among the biggest names – followed a similar pattern, although by the end of the decade pioneering promoters such as Larry Parnes (jokingly known in the business as 'Mr Parnes, Shillings and Pence') were staging all-pop line-ups.

Promoters like Parnes and Arthur Howes usually used small local printers – or regional firms, such as Arthurs Press of Gloucestershire or the Kent-based Hastings Printing Company – to produce their posters. Most of the 'variety'-style posters – also known as 'boxing match' posters, as they resembled bills promoting boxing matches – were printed letterpress, with the 'design' element, such as it was, being provided by the in-house compositor whose job it was to assemble the individual letters in the 'forme' from which the posters would be printed.

But in the early sixties, as smaller clubs opened in towns and cities across Britain with the onset of the rhythm and blues boom, gig poster design started to evolve: local promoters, requiring only small numbers of posters and flyers, began to commission work from local commercial artists, who would hand-draw their own type and often silk-screen-print the posters themselves. Compared to the rigid format of the letterpress-printed 'boxing match' posters, the resulting designs were individual and inventive in their use of colour and type – despite the fact that the artists who produced them rarely had any formal training in graphic design.

Such artists would almost certainly have been aware, even if only subliminally, of the strong body of British poster art produced pre- and post-World War II by graphic artists such as James Fitton and Tom Eckersley, who were commissioned by London Underground, Shell and the General Post Office, among others. But even if the artists working outside this more formal poster-art tradition had possessed the training required to produce posters in the 'fine art' mould, they would have been severely constrained, since the gig promoters they were working for needed the posters quickly – and they wanted them produced to a tight budget.

However, with Britain's post-war recovery came a growing prosperity – and educational opportunities for the nation's youth. In 1954, for example, Eckersley joined the London College of Printing and went on to establish Britain's first graphic design course. It was thus the next wave of graphic designers, emerging from the art colleges, who would take British rock 'n' roll poster art to new levels in the sixties and after.

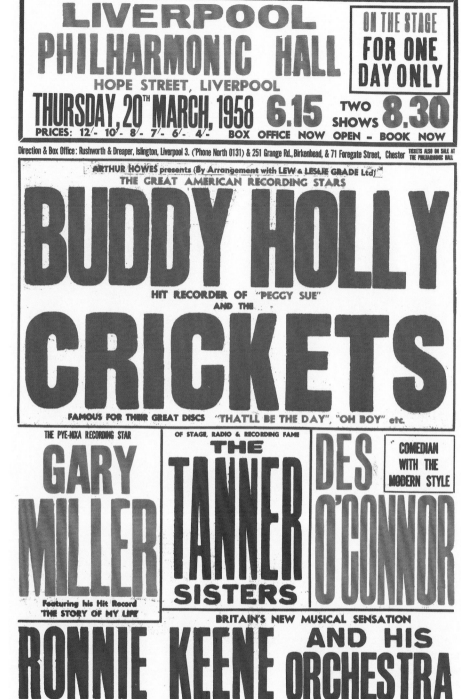

The poster (above) for a 1949 concert put on by Combined Services Entertainment – an organization set up in 1946 to provide entertainment for British armed forces personnel – was probably hand-lettered and silk-screen-printed. Ivy Benson and her all-girl band were a popular attraction in World War II and through to the early fifties.

The Buddy Holly and the Crickets poster (right) advertises one of the earliest UK tours by an American pop group. Although none of the supporting acts in the 'package' (put together by promoter Arthur Howes), could be described as rock 'n' roll, the *Melody Maker* review of the first concert of the tour – staged at the Trocadero in London's Elephant and Castle on March 1, ran: 'The out-dated Variety halls could learn a lot from these teenage coast-to-coast tours . . . This is one of the best package shows to be presented for approval of teenage audiences. And judging by the reaction on Saturday, the teenagers appreciate it'. The poster was printed letterpress, using mostly wooden display type locked into a metal frame called a 'forme'.

Above left
The Canteen, London, October 1949

Above right
Liverpool Philharmonic Hall, March 1958

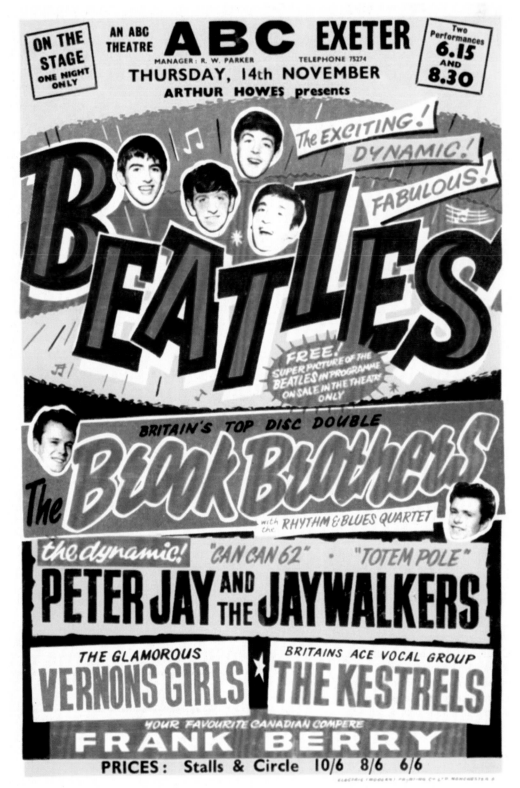

In 1961, Liverpool rock groups still shared the bill with traditional jazz bands at many gigs. This 'Riverboat Shuffle' gig promoted by the Cavern Club (above left) featured Mr Acker Bilk's Paramount Jazz Band, with the Beatles supporting. The poster was designed by Tony Booth, who produced many posters for Brian Epstein and other promoters in the sixties. Booth comments: 'If only about ten [posters] were required, I would do them all by hand, but larger quantities would go to a local silk-screen printer for bulk printing and distribution.' This poster (as with the other examples of Booth's work shown in this chapter) was hand-lettered on machine-glazed poster paper; the poster's size was Double Crown (30 inches by 20 inches).

By the time of the Beatles' winter tour of 1963 (which took in Exeter among other venues), the artwork style was loosening up with some energetic graphics. The freer use of colour and the inclusion of the photos in this poster suggest that it might be an early example of offset-litho printing, as does the name of the printer – the Electric Modern Printing Co. of Manchester.

Above left
Liverpool [Tony Booth],
August 1961

Above right
ABC Theatre, Exeter,
June 1963

A poster advertising the first of the famed 'Operation "Big Beat"' series of concerts at the Tower Ballroom, New Brighton (above left), organized by Liverpool promoter Sam Leach. Like the Riverboat Shuffle poster opposite, this was designed by Tony Booth. Booth had attended the Wallasey School of Arts and Crafts until the age of 18; after completing his National Service in 1953, he started work as a commercial artist at a Liverpool advertising agency, and continued in that trade until he retired.

Unlike the more sophisticated design of the Arthur Howes Exeter concert poster shown on the opposite page, the poster above right, advertising another Howes show at Torquay in the same year, reverts to the rigid template of the 'boxing poster' style. The compositor who assembled the type for this letterpress-printed poster was clearly working under pressure, as he (almost never 'she') used a haphazard mixture of border rule styles – some of the rules have mitred corners, while others have squared ends, plus some are joined up to create a solid 'box' rule, while others are not.

Above left
Tower Ballroom, New Brighton
[Tony Booth],
November 1961

Above right
Princess Theatre, Torquay,
August 1963

PRINCESS THEATRE TORQUAY TEL. 7527

General Manager for the Org. A. F. Roberts

SUNDAY CONCERTS

18th AUG. at 6 and 8.30 p.m.

BERNARD DELFONT

by arrangement with ARTHUR HOWES presents

Britain's Fabulous Disc Stars

THE BEATLES

LIVERPOOL'S LATEST THE FOURMOST RECORDING GROUP

THE KESTRELS
ACE VOCAL GROUP

LYNNE PERRI BOB BAIN OUR COMPERE BARRY BARNETT

HAROLD COLLINS and the PRINCESS THEATRE ORCHESTRA

SUNDAY, 25th AUG. DANNY WILLIAMS

Stalls & Circle 10/6 8/6 6/- BOX OFFICE open 10 a.m. daily

HASTINGS PRINTING COMPANY PORTLAND PLACE HASTINGS

AZENA BALLROOM GLEADLESS
SATURDAY 12TH FEB. 1963
Live! ON STAGE
FROM THE CAVERN CLUB
THE BEATLES
No.1 Single "PLEASE PLEASE ME"
Presented by STRINGFELLOW BROS.
Tickets 6! OBTAINABLE FROM THE BLACK CAT CLUB

At the "CASSANOVA CLUB"
SAMPSON AND BARLOW'S FABULOUS
NEW BALLROOM
LONDON ROAD OPPOSITE ODEON Cinema
Valentine's Night
Rock Ball
TUESDAY 14th. FEB
7·30/midnight
4 Rompin' Stompin' Bands!
STARRING THE ORIGINATORS OF 'THE ATOM BEAT' The Sensational Beatles
ROCKIN THE SOUND WAVES THE CASSANOVA BIG THREE
RORY STORM and the HURRICANES
and Introducing MARK PETERS and the CYCLONES
LICENSED BAR AND BUFFET UNTIL 11·0 p.m
TICKETS 4'6 (INCLUDING REFRESHMENTS) ON SALE AT Rushworth's · Lewis's · Cranes

The 1961 poster (right) was commissioned from Tony Booth by Sam Leach to promote his 'Valentine's Night Rock Ball' at the Cassanova Club in Liverpool. The poster bills the Beatles as 'the originators of "The Atom Beat"', a reference to the group's raucous onstage foot-stomping. Booth notes that 'The style of lettering I used on the posters was known as "Cartoon or Freestyle", which became popular in the early fifties and was influenced by American newspaper ads for Buick Cars.'

The simple black and white poster (above left) from two years later was designed and silk-screen-printed by Colin Duffield – 'Sheffield's first sixties pop poster artist', in Mojo Club archivist Dave Manvell's words. The poster was in fact produced after the gig, as a souvenir of the Beatles' Azena Ballroom appearance. It contains three errors: although the group did play the Azena Ballroom on February 12, that day was a Tuesday, not a Saturday; 'Please Please Me', released in January 1963, did not get to the #1 spot until February 22; and the familiar 'dropped T' on the Beatles' logo was not adopted until May or June of that year.

Above left
Azena Ballroom,
Gleadless, Sheffield
[Colin Duffield],
mid-1963

Above right
Cassanova Club, Liverpool
[Tony Booth],
February 1961

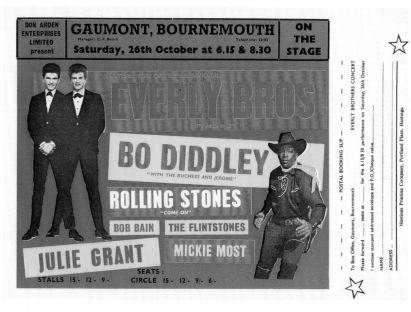

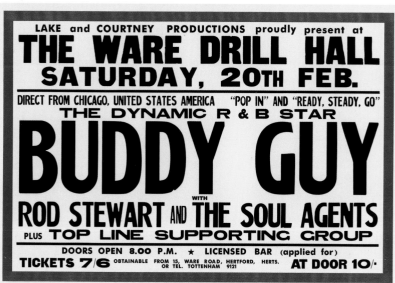

A flyer advertising a Bournemouth concert (top left) by the Everly Brothers/Bo Diddley touring package, assembled by promoter Don Arden in 1963; the tour manager was Peter Grant, future Led Zeppelin manager. This was the first major UK tour for the Rolling Stones, who are listed third on the bill. Flyers, which were smaller in size, could easily be printed landscape, but it was less common for posters, such as the one advertising bluesman Buddy Guy's first UK tour (below left), to be produced in this format.

The Screaming Lord Sutch poster (above) was designed and silk-screen-printed by Colin Duffield. A signwriter by trade, like most poster artists of the era Duffield had no formal art or graphic design training. The Sheffield artist comments that he 'just came up with' the idea for the 'horned savage' face.

Top left
Gaumont Cinema,
Bournemouth,
October 1963

Below left
The Drill Hall, Ware,
Hertfordshire,
February 1965

Above right
Co-op Unity Hall, Wakefield
[Colin Duffield],
January 1963

THE JAZZ CONNECTION

Although the big stars of the beat and R&B boom that dominated British popular music in the first half of the 1960s toured the country playing large venues – such as cinemas, theatres, ballrooms and civic halls (often as part of 'packaged' shows assembled by promoters such as Larry Parnes and Arthur Howes) – the core of the scene was to be found in a network of local clubs, many of which had started life as jazz venues in the fifties.

From the late 1940s, in the wake of World War II, jazz had become increasingly popular, and throughout the fifties it was the trendy alternative to chart-driven pop music. Indeed, rock 'n' roll and pop generally were anathema to most jazz fans. It's ironic, therefore, that the jazz haunts that sprang up in every town and city throughout the UK would become the backbone of the sixties' rock revolution.

Pioneering jazz clubs in London included the Club Eleven (originally dubbed the Metropolitan Bopera House!) and Downbeat, both opening in 1948, and the Flamingo, which started life in 1952 and became a key R&B venue in the early sixties. But one of the first jazz venues to open in London after the war was the Canteen, run by the Combined Services Entertainment organization, which was established in 1946 to provide entertainment for off-duty members of the armed forces. The vibrant design of its American-influenced posters and handbills was an early portent of the impact that jazz (and subsequently rock 'n' roll) would have on an otherwise drab and austere Britain during those postwar years.

Cellar clubs were particularly fashionable in the fifties jazz scene, evoking the bohemian feel of Parisian 'Left Bank' haunts; indeed, the Cavern Club in Liverpool, situated in a dank warehouse basement, was inspired by La Huchette, a Latin Quarter club in the French capital that is still open today. The Cavern played host to jazz outfits every night of the week from its opening in 1958 until rock 'n' roll groups,

including the Beatles, started appearing alongside the jazz artists from around 1960. By 1962, the club was almost exclusively a rock venue.

A similar change occurred in clubs up and down the country, from famous locales such as London's Marquee (located in a basement under a cinema in Oxford Street when it first opened in 1958) and Ken Colyer's Jazz Club (a.k.a. Studio 51, where the Rolling Stones played their first London dates), to scores of regional venues. Even the Humphrey Lyttelton Club – which, as the Feldman Swing Club, was considered Britain's first-ever jazz venue when it opened in 1942 – became the 100 Club with a blues guitar as its logo.

Unlike the bigger ballrooms and civic halls, all of these venues were independently run – usually by local entrepreneurs and/or promoters – and as a consequence they generated their own publicity material. Some had developed a distinctive 'house style' when they were jazz venues, like the Cavern with its cartoon 'cave-dweller' trademark on local ads and membership cards (the latter were designed by Tony Booth). Similarly, the National Jazz Federation that ran the Marquee (named after the circus-tent decor that dated from its previous incarnation as the Marquee Ballroom) adopted a jazz-style trumpet-on-chair logo. This logo continued to appear on all its promotions through the sixties, including the annual Jazz/Blues and Rock Festival that was the forerunner of today's Reading Festival.

As a consequence of the early sixties rhythm and blues boom, which might be said to have truly begun in the Marquee in 1962 with Alexis Korner's twice-weekly R&B nights, even more clubs sprang up in towns and cities across the UK. Many adopted blues-inspired names, such as Peter Stringfellow's Mojo (later, the King Mojo) in Sheffield and Richmond's Crawdaddy, and such clubs often developed a graphic style of their own. British R&B, like jazz before it, launched itself with a purely cult following in 'underground' clubs, but would go on to change the course of popular music in the first half of the sixties.

'We noticed that the management was no longer hiring a jazz band to play during our interval . . . we returned from the pub to find the small stage cluttered with amplification.'
Jazz singer George Melly on playing the Cavern, *Revolt Into Style* (Allen Lane, 1970)

Above left
The Canteen, London,
October 1950

Top right
National Jazz Festival,
Richmond,
August 1963

Below right
The Cavern, Liverpool,
June 1962

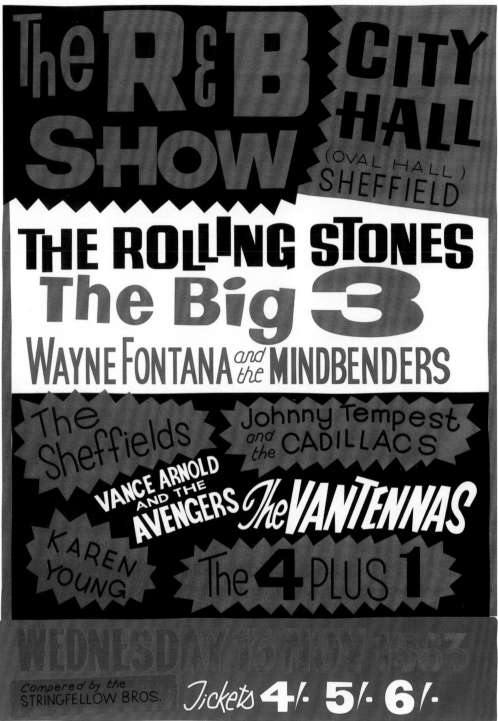

The 1963 poster by Colin Duffield (left) advertises a Peter Stringfellow promotion, headlined by the Rolling Stones. Duffield produced many of Stringfellow's posters, using the silk-screen process. Each letter would be cut out with a fine craft knife, and the resulting stencils laid on the mesh 'bed' of the silk-screen machine. The different solid colours would then be washed over the bed, creating vivid posters like this one. When they became more generally available in the early 1960s, Duffield and other artists increasingly used products such as Profilm (an early version of masking film), which obviated the need to draw each letter by hand, saving time and money.

Alongside is a typical line-up from the Larry Parnes stable of imaginatively named rockers, including Vince Eager, Dickie Pride and Billy Fury. Despite Parnes' implication that many of the artists in his show were American, all except for Davy Jones were British. Tony Gardner wrote that Parnes was the first to 'perfect . . . the concept of the package tour, in which his stable of stars toured the country in a bus, playing one-night stands at theatres wherever an audience could be packed in'.

Above left
City Hall, Sheffield
[Colin Duffield],
November 1963

Above right
Britannia Theatre,
Great Yarmouth,
March 1961

A 1965 Animals poster (right) announces a gig at the Swindon Locarno, and demonstrates that – despite the fact that it was now the middle of the 'Swinging Sixties' – some poster styles had hardly changed at all. Likewise, a 1966 poster for 'The Big Star Show' at the Royal Aquarium Theatre in Great Yarmouth (above left) would have been a straightforward, no-frills job for the typesetter, with its simple use of sans serif lettering and limited range of colours. The selection of acts for the show – from Gerry and the Pacemakers to 'The Marionettes' – was clearly designed to appeal to the widest possible audience; it was, essentially, a variety show.

Above left
Royal Aquarium Theatre,
Great Yarmouth,
June 1966

Above right
Locarno, Swindon,
March 1965

LOCARNO
7.45—11.00 6/6 Members 6/- Lounge. Bar

THURSDAY, MAR. 25
TOP 10 STARS !
THE ANIMALS
"DON'T LET ME BE MISUNDERSTOOD"

THE SOLE SAVAGES
FEATURING
PAUL DEAN

THE WHO

MARIANNE FAITHFULL

SOLOMON BURKE

ZOOT MONEY

10/6 ALL DAY
2.0—11.30 P.M.

UXBRIDGE BLUES
AND
FOLK FESTIVAL
SAT. JUNE 19
UXBRIDGE SHOW

NEAR SWIMMING
AND STATION

an

THE BIRDS

DAVE WHITTLING
FOLK SINGER

RAY MARTIN
GROUP

WEATHER GOOD - OPEN AIR !!
LICENSED BARS !!

WEATHER B

GRAND EVENING FEST

TICKET PRICES: **7/6** AFTERNOON OR EVENING AND **10/6** AFTERNO

Available from Georgian Club, High St., Cowley, Uxbridge, Sat. Nights Only
Farenwide Travel Agency, 588, Uxbridge Rd., Hayes 6593
Or direct by Post from the Treasurer, 76, Fairholme Cres., Hayes

Blue Moon Club, Church Rd., Ha
Barnard and Warren, Bakers Rd.,
ALL AMPLIFICATION BY JIM MARSHAL

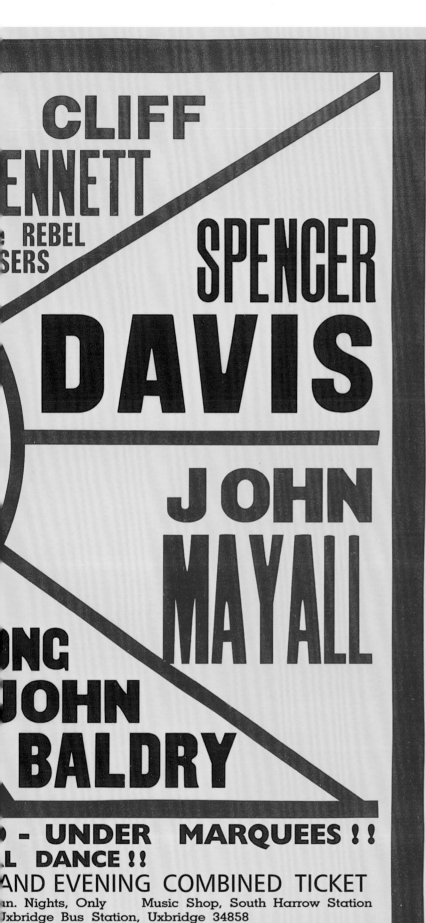

**CLIFF
ENNETT**

e **REBEL**
SERS

**SPENCER
DAVIS**

**JOHN
MAYALL**

NG
JOHN
BALDRY

– UNDER MARQUEES !!

L **DANCE !!**

AND EVENING COMBINED TICKET

n. Nights, Only   Music Shop, South Harrow Station
Uxbridge Bus Station, Uxbridge 34858
SUPPLIED BY ROSE MORRIS and CO., LTD., N.W.5

THE MOST FAMOUS CLUB IN EUROPE
**BRISTOL CHINESE R & B JAZZ CLUB
EVERY TUESDAY**
at the
CORN EXCHANGE · CORN ST.

TUESDAY, 18th MAY   Top Recording Group "Decca"
THEM

TUESDAY, 18th MAY   R & B at its Rawest
SPENCER DAVIES

TUESDAY, 25th MAY
THE BO STREET RUNNERS

TUESDAY, 1st JUNE
THE BIRDS

TUESDAY, 8th JUNE   from America-Top Blues Artist
JOHN LEE HOOKER
plus **THE COPS AND ROBBERS**

Nurses Half-Price   Students Admitted on Student Cards
Crocodile Sandwiches   Fly Lice   Uncle Bonny

Left
Uxbridge Blues
and Folk Festival,
June 1965

Above
Chinese R&B Jazz Club,
Bristol,
May 1965

This poster (left) for the second day of the Uxbridge Blues and Folk Festival is unremarkable in graphic terms, but its 'rising sun' format, like the bands on offer, is a taste of exciting things to come. The Bristol Chinese R&B Jazz Club – held in the Corn Exchange every Tuesday – was one of the more bizarre venues on the mid-1960s circuit; below the otherwise impressive line-up of forthcoming acts, it also proclaims 'Nurses Half-Price,' 'Crocodile Sandwiches' and 'Fly Lice'!

TOWN HALL
CASTLE CIRCUS. TORQUAY.
TORBAY MANAGEMENTS PRESENTS A
SUMMER SPECTACULAR
STARRING THE DEDICATED FOLLOWERS OF FASHION
THE KINKS
LATEST No. 1 HIT "SUNNY AFTERNOON"
**THE TRAVELLERS ★ THE LAST·TIK·BAND
THE PACKAGE DEAL ★ THE REACTION**
PLUS FABULOUS MOD FASHION PARADE
TUESDAY 16TH AUG.
8 - 1 A.M. LATE LICENSED BAR TILL 12.30 A.M. TICKETS 10/-
ADVANCE TICKETS FROM John Conway, Mens Fashion Shop Abbey Road, Torquay. 27322
or send P.O. and S.A.E. to Impact House, 31, Market Street. Torquay.
Promoted by L.M.D. ENTERTAINMENTS LTD. Torquay 22585

COMING SATURDAY 20th AUG.
THE WHO

TOWN HALL TORQUAY
Come Dancing in the Club Atmosphere Ballroom
with Low Lighting and Two Band Stands
SUMMER RAVE
"Hi! Ho! Silver Lining" its
THE
JEFF BECK
GROUP
THE SABRES | THE INSEXTS
Featuring the Fantastic VICKY | with Fab Soul Vocalist GINO
SATURDAY 15th JULY
7.30 | 11.45 p.m. | LATE LICENSED BAR | Tickets 8/6
Advance Tickets from John Conway, Men's Fashion Shop,
Abbey Road, Torquay 27322
Presented by L.M.D. Entertainments Ltd.

Coming Tuesday 10th July	Coming Saturday 22nd July
MANFRED MANN	**BONZO DOG DO DAH DAH BAND**

CLUB NOREIK
HIGH RD., TOTTENHAM, N.15
SAT. MAR. 13
THE WHO
PLUS
THE CANDLES
ADMISSION 7/6
ARTHURS, WOODCHESTER, STROUD

Some of the venues in British seaside resorts – particularly town halls run by the local authorities – were the country's most conservative in their publicity material. While elsewhere the early hints of psychedelia were creeping into rock 'n' roll graphics, bills like these headed by the Kinks in 1966, and Jeff Beck in 1967, looked like nothing had changed since the 1950s. The poster for the Who advertises a gig at Club Noreik – a famous North London venue that had been converted from a bingo hall.

Above left
Town Hall, Torquay,
August 1966

Above right
Town Hall, Torquay,
July 1967

Below right
Club Noreik, Tottenham,
London,
March 1965

WEST END JIVING

STARRING

THE FEDERALS   THE BEL-AIRS   THE DETOURS

AT

5, LEICESTER PLACE, LEICESTER SQ., LONDON, W.C.2

LUXURIOUS BALLROOM

8–11.30   ADMISSION 4/6   REFRESHMENTS

ENQUIRIES:–3, THORNEY HEDGE ROAD, CHISWICK, W.4

TAYLOR ENTERTAINMENTS IN CONJUNCTION WITH COMMERCIAL ENTERTAINMENTS LIMITED

FOX & GOOSE HOTEL

HANGER LANE, EALING W.5

JIVING & TWISTING

FRIDAYS

FEATURING THE DYNAMIC

"DETOURS"

7.30–11.00 P.M.   4/- ADMISSION

LICENSED BALLROOM BAR

BUSES—83, 187 TO DOOR 112, 105 TWO MINUTES   TRAINS—HANGER LANE, PARK ROYAL

COMMENCING FRIDAY, 11TH JAN.

Top
Club Druane, Notre Dame
Church Hall, Leicester Square,
London,
August 1963

Above left
Fox & Goose Hotel, Ealing,
London,
January 1963

These rare landscape posters announce 'jiving' dates by the Detours, who would later become the Who. Jiving was American rock 'n' roll dancing that became popular in British dance halls in the 1950s; new jiving moves were broadcast to UK viewers twice a week on pop TV show *Ready Steady Go!* When Chubby Checker's 'Let's Twist Again' hit the charts in 1961, the new dance craze was 'The Twist' and in the US twist instructions were given out with every record: 'Imagine you are stubbing out a cigarette with both feet whilst drying your back with a towel.'

02

READY STEADY MOD!

ART INTO POP

With the UK beat and R&B boom of the early to mid-1960s came a burgeoning circuit of clubs, such as the Cavern in Liverpool and London's Marquee, both of which had previously thrived as jazz venues. While the big-name pop groups continued to tour the 2,000-seater cinemas and theatres (the Beatles had played their final Cavern date in August 1963), hundreds of cellar clubs and rooms over pubs played host to an army of beat and blues groups following in the wake of their success – these provided a launch-pad for up-and-coming bands, from the Who to the Jimi Hendrix Experience.

With the emergence of this booming club scene came a new-found appreciation of the importance of poster design. Some promoters, such as the Ricky-Tick club's Philip Hayward and John Mansfield – recognizing the value of a bold, striking image as a way of pulling in the punters – commissioned specific artists to create a trademark style for their venues. Others, like the Yardbirds' manager, Giorgio Gomelsky, asked designers to create distinctive 'logos' that identified their bands on posters, publicity handouts and, eventually, record covers. And in the case of the Who, a close

collaboration between Pete Townshend and promoter Richard Barnes produced the 'mod' graphic style – reflecting the clean, modernist approach of Reid Miles' designs for Blue Note records – associated with the image of the group. Despite this evolution, examples of the old 'variety' or 'boxing' style of posters nevertheless continued to be produced, even in the latter years of the decade.

From the world of 'serious' painting, the pop art movement was increasingly reflected in British popular culture. Famously, students from London's Royal College of Art were responsible for the targets-and-union-jack imagery of TV's rock flagship *Ready Steady Go!*, a pop iconography not lost on Pete Townshend (himself an ex-art student) as the main creative force of the Who.

Club posters of the period began to appropriate this new 'mod' symbolism as the (usually anonymous) artists broke away from the earlier rigid templates. It was a move to a more self-consciously 'artistic' stance on the part of the designers, which would subsequently find full expression in the sumptuous visual excesses of the psychedelic era.

TOP of the POPS

HILLSIDE BALLROOM
ROSS ROAD, HEREFORD

FRI. 13TH DEC.
9 p.m. to 12.30 a.m.
COME ON! to our
XMAS PARTY with the

ROLLING STONES

PLUS

THE VALIANTS

ADM. 7/6   REFRESHMENTS
LICENSED BAR (app. for)
**LATE BUSES INTO AND AROUND TOWN PLUS MANY LATE COACHES
IF YOU LIVE OUTSIDE HEREFORD PLEASE SEE YOUR LOCAL COACH OPERATOR**

LOCARNO Liverpool
THURSDAY · 14TH FEB. 7·30 – 11·30

We present your Valentines

The BEATLES

**PLUS
FREE GIFTS
FOR THE FIRST
500 LADIES**

**ALL
PAY
AT
DOOR 3/6**

Above left
Hillside Ballroom, Hereford,
December 1963

Above right
Locarno Ballroom, Liverpool
[Tony Booth],
February 1963

Dance halls across the country, which had flourished in every town and city since the 1920s, moved away from their strictly ballroom-dancing policy in the early sixties to accommodate the demand for beat groups such as the Rolling Stones. Their advertising, too, which was usually produced by local commercial artists and/or printers, began to exhibit a new flair, as with the Hillside Ballroom poster shown left. Many of the most famous bands of the sixties played at this Hereford venue. The original Mott the Hoople singer, Stan Tippins, was at this concert, and noted that the Hillside 'was only half full; most people [at the concert] didn't know who [the band] were . . . [but] They were fantastic'.

The night before their Hillside appearance, the Stones had played at the Locarno in Liverpool – a hugely popular venue in Liverpool in the sixties, mainly as a dance hall. This Tony Booth poster advertises a Sam Leach-arranged Beatles gig at the venue on Valentine's Night, 1963. Booth notes that 'About a hundred [of the posters] were silk-screened for local distribution, together with the usual thousand matching flyers that would be distributed to local shops'.

BRIAN EPSTEIN presents
THE BEATLES
Christmas Show

THE BEATLES

BILLY J. KRAMER THE DAKOTAS

ROLF HARRIS

THE FOURMOST

CILLA BLACK

TOMMY QUICKLY

THE BARRON KNIGHTS
FEATURING
DUKE D' MOND

DEVISED AND PRODUCED BY PETER YOLLAND

FINSBURY PARK ASTORIA
from Tuesday 24 December 1963 to Saturday 11 January 1964.

Booking Controller ....)		(.......... GEORGE PINCHES
Production Director ....)	FOR THE RANK ORGANISATION	(............ STAN FISHMAN
Stage Director ....)	(THEATRE DIVISION)	(................ BILL WEST
Stage Manager ....)		(........... MIKE McKEAGH
Assistant Stage Manager ....)	FOR NEMS PRESENTATIONS	(......... KENNY ASHCROFT
Press Representative ....)		(............. TONY BARROW

THE HIGH NUMBERS

EVERY TUESDAY 3/6

RAILWAY HOTEL HARROW & WEALDSTONE !

ST. GEORGE'S HALL EXETER

"67's 'Tickle me' BALL"

FEATURING THE

alan price SET

PLUS! THE IN·SECT

PLUS! 'EMPTY VESSELS'

FRIDAY 17 NOV

TICKETS 10: FROM 'MINNS' PARK ST or 12/- AT DOOR

FULLY LICENSED BAR UNTIL 12·30

NO PASSOUTS * DANCING 8·30–1·AM

The 'Beatles Christmas Show' poster (opposite) is something of a hybrid, retaining elements of the old variety style but with a cleaner, more balanced use of typography and colour. The 1967 Alan Price Set gig poster (above) also reveals a mix of design influences, with its slightly 'mod' bold block of colour in the centre and variety poster elements.

The Who were formed in February 1964, having previously been known as the Detours; they changed their name to the High Numbers briefly during the summer of that year, at which point they had the residency at the Railway Hotel, Harrow (left), before reverting to the Who a few months later. The hotel club was run by Pete Townshend's friend Richard Barnes, who 'not only designed [this] poster but printed and fly-posted it . . . Townshend and I shared a flat in Ealing that had six or seven rooms . . . I took the biggest room as a silk-screen-printing studio and designed and printed posters, mainly for the Railway Hotel club . . . I copied the design [for this poster] from an *Observer* or *Sunday Times* poster I'd seen, which we thought was quite 'mod' . . . When we started fly posting silk-screen-printed posters [like this] alongside the letterpress [gig] posters . . . that were ubiquitous at the time, the colours looked [very] strong and vivid.'

Above left
Railway Hotel,
Harrow & Wealdstone
[Richard Barnes],
Summer 1964

Above right
St George's Hall, Exeter,
November 1967

Opposite
Programme, Beatles
Christmas Show, London,
December 1963

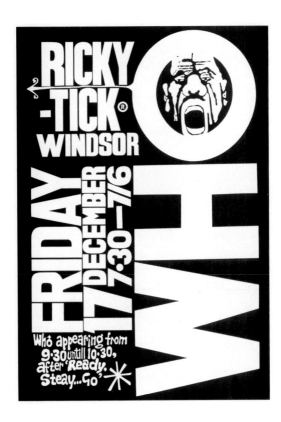

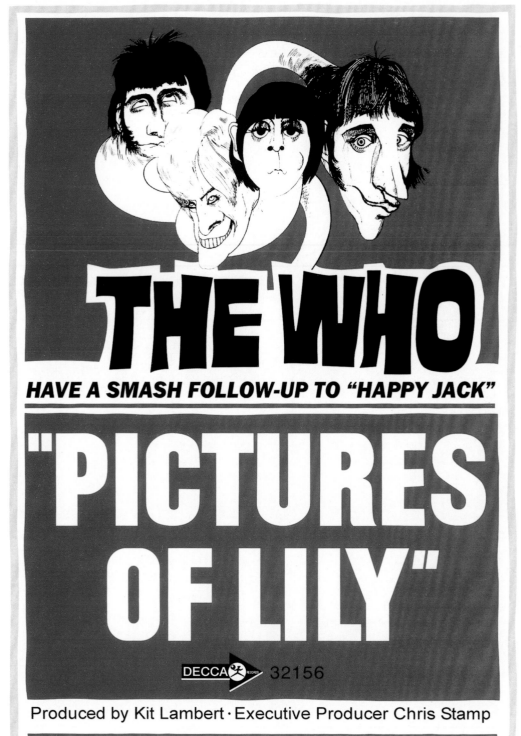

When the Who played the Ricky-Tick club in Windsor on Friday, December 17, 1965, they arrived just after appearing on the *Ready Steady Go!* TV show. The first Ricky-Tick club was established in a pub (the Star & Garter, now demolished) in Windsor in 1962 by promoters John Mansfield and Philip Hayward; in 1964 it moved to a nearby mansion, Clewer Mead. While this remained the main venue, over the next four years Mansfield and Hayward put on Ricky-Tick gigs at some 27 different locations across southern England – providing a launch pad for some of the biggest bands of the era. The distinctive 'screaming face' logo that appeared on all the Ricky-Tick posters from the spring of 1963 was designed by Bob McGrath (a.k.a. Hogsnort Rupert), at the time a student at Farnham Art College. Mansfield notes that, initially, McGrath printed the posters himself but that, as the promoters needed 'more and more posters . . . [McGrath] said he would cut out the design in Stenplex. We then had to iron that on to silk-screens and print the posters ourselves. [McGrath] helped us with the first two batches and then we were on our own.'

The caricatures of the Who on the promotional poster (right) for their 1967 single 'Pictures Of Lily' were far more intriguing than much of the earlier promo art put out by Decca and the other big record companies.

Above left
Ricky-Tick, Windsor
[Bob McGrath],
December 1965

Above right
'Pictures Of Lily'
record promotion,
April 1967

Designed by Brian Pike, an advertising associate of the Who manager Kit Lambert, this 'Maximum R&B' poster advertised the group's 1964–65 Tuesday night residency at the Marquee club. Lambert coined the phrase 'Maximum R&B' and spent a princely £300 on printing posters and flyers to advertise the event. On the Who's first night, only 30 fans braved the pouring rain to see the band. However, within three weeks the club night had broken house attendance records, previously set by the Yardbirds and Manfred Mann.

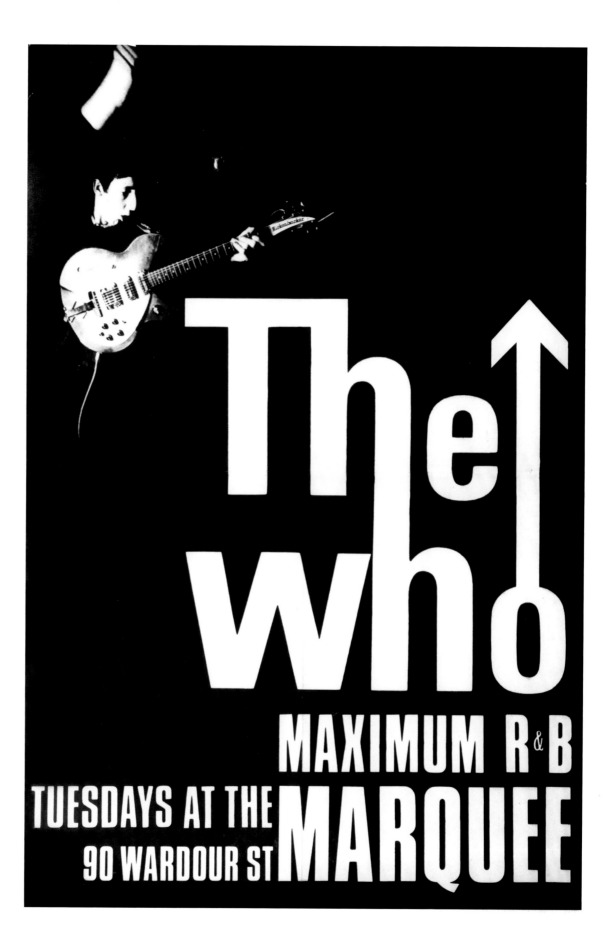

Above right
The Marquee, Wardour Street,
London [Brian Pike],
November 1964

POP INTO ART

The pop art movement's roots can be traced back as far as 1947, when the British artist Eduardo Paolozzi created a collage from popular American magazine cut-outs entitled *I Was A Rich Man's Plaything*, featuring a pin-up glamour model, a Coca-Cola bottle and the word 'Pop!' emerging from the barrel of a gun. In 1952, Paolozzi was a co-founder of the Independent Group of young UK artists, and would later tutor the Beatles' original bass player Stuart Sutcliffe after he'd left the group to study painting in Hamburg. The group developed the idea that the images and techniques of popular culture – advertising, comic strips, science fiction, movies and so forth – could be appropriated for 'serious' art.

As the movement took off, one of the earliest works to be considered 'pop art' was another collage of images taken from everyday life, *Just What Is It That Makes Today's Homes So Different, So Appealing?*, produced in 1956 by the painter Richard Hamilton. Hamilton was also an influential teacher, most notably at King's College, Newcastle upon Tyne, between 1953 and 1966, where his students included the Liverpool painter (and later leader of the Liverpool Scene rock group) Adrian Henri and Roxy Music's Bryan Ferry. Ferry's fellow students included Nick De Ville, with whom Ferry would collaborate on Roxy's album covers and stage image. Richard Hamilton's most direct involvement with the world of pop music, however, came in 1968, when he designed the minimalist sleeve for the Beatles' so-called 'White Album', and the poster/collage that came with the package.

Meanwhile, in the US – the source of much of the UK's pop imagery – pop artists were taking a different course. Painters such as Jasper Johns, with his images of flattened flags and targets, James Rosenquist, with his evocations of the vast canvasses of billboard art, and Roy Lichtenstein's parodies of 'true romance' comic strips, were more inclined to adopt a questioning rather than a romanticized approach to their own country's culture.

Equally inspired by both American and intrinsically British pop culture, Peter Blake emerged at the beginning of the 1960s as a major name in pop art. His work was first recognized in the Young Contemporaries exhibition in 1961, alongside that of David Hockney, and, with other young painters, was featured in a 1962 BBC television documentary

Pop Goes the Easel, which established pop art in the mainstream media.

Blake would become best known for his cover of the Beatles' *Sgt. Pepper* album, but other forays into sleeve design have included the Who's *Face Dances* in 1981, *Stanley Road* by Paul Weller (1995) and the Ian Dury tribute album *Brand New Boots and Panties* in 2001. Blake was Dury's tutor at the Royal College of Art in the mid-1960s, when the college was a hotbed of creativity and had a direct bearing on the rock scene's assimilation of pop art imagery. Students from the college were employed to design the sets for a new weekly rock 'n' roll TV show launched in 1963, *Ready Steady Go!* One of them, Clive Arrowsmith, would become the programme's art director before embarking on a subsequent career as a highly successful photographer (his credentials in the latter role included Paul McCartney's Wings album *Band On The Run*). The pop iconography on *Ready Steady Go!* – targets, Union Jack flags, 'road sign' arrows – drew on Blake, Johns and the rest of the pop art fraternity, as well as other image makers, from the 'mod' fashions of Mary Quant, to the (mainly black and white) 'op art' optical illusion paintings of Bridget Riley.

By the mid-1960s, the style had permeated into every corner of the popular media, from fashion to advertising, magazine graphics, and cult TV shows such as *Batman*, *The Prisoner* and *The Man From U.N.C.L.E.* And, not least, the world of music, where new 'mod' bands like the Who, the Action and the Move – and the hundreds of clubs where they cut their teeth – were quick to pick up on the potency of pop art imagery.

The Who, most notably, adopted the targets, arrows and flags in their attire and publicity graphics, which came as no surprise, given that Pete Townshend was a former art student. Townshend had studied at Ealing School of Art under Gustav Metzger, the pioneer of 'auto-destructive art', whose influence was manifestly evident in Townshend's 'guitar-smashing' act on stage. Townshend was only one of a generation of British rock musicians who had come out of the art schools; other artists-turned-musicians included Ray Davies, John Lennon, Eric Clapton and Keith Richards.

By the late sixties, the hard-edged logos and primary colours of pop art had given way to the swirling graphics of psychedelia. However, the influence of pop art would prove fundamental and enduring, and marked the first time that pop had come into art, and art into pop.

'Popular, transient, expendable, low cost, mass-produced, young, witty, sexy, gimmicky, glamorous and Big Business.'
Richard Hamilton's definition of pop art, 1957

Above
Paul Weller's *Stanley Road* album cover [Peter Blake], June 1995

The Birdcage in Portsmouth was typical of the many clubs around the country that designed their own posters and publicity material. The examples here include two featuring the Who, the earlier of which (top left) incorporates a 'pop art'-type target, typical of the group during that period. At the time of the Pink Floyd poster above left, the band line-up included Syd Barrett, Nick Mason, Roger Waters and Rick Wright.

Top left
Birdcage, Portsmouth,
December 1965

Above left
Birdcage, Portsmouth,
April 1967

Above right
Birdcage, Portsmouth,
February 1967

CITY HALL - NEWCASTLE
MONDAY 30th OCTOBER at 6.00 & 8.30

KENNEDY STREET ENTERPRISES LTD. and PETER WALSH Present

THE WHO

TRAFFIC

THE HERD

The MARMALADE

Compère RAY CAMERON

★★ SPECIAL GUEST STARS ★★

THE TREMELOES

TICKETS 12/6 10/6 8/6 7/6 5/-

Book at Cooks Ltd.

Birmingham Theatre

ONE NIGHT ONLY — TWO PERFORMANCES

Sunday, 17th November at 5.30 and 8.00 p.m.

THE WHO

THE CRAZY WORLD OF ARTHUR BROWN

SPECIAL GUEST STARS

THE SMALL FACES

THE MINDBENDERS

TICKETS : 15/- 12/6 10/6 7/6

Top
City Hall, Newcastle,
October 1967

Above left
Birmingham Theatre,
Birmingham,
November 1968

Two-performances-a-night package shows featuring four or five rock acts continued to be popular into the late 1960s. Although the two posters above owed their basic layouts to the 'variety bill' tradition, it is interesting to note that the designers decided to bill each group in a separate – and sometimes quirky – typographic style.

SAVOY - A.B.C.   EXETER

| On The Stage | Manager : R. W. PARKER   Tele. 75274
 SUNDAY, 5th DECEMBER, 1965
 5 - 15   TWO PERFORMANCES   7 - 45 | One Night Only |

MARQUEE PRODUCTIONS LTD.
in association with the
GEORGE COOPER ORGANISATION LTD. present

THE MARQUEE SHOW

MANFRED MANN

First Appearance of
'POP SATIRISTS'

PAUL & BARRY RYAN   THE SCAFFOLD

FROM U.S.A.

INEZ AND CHARLIE FOX

MARK LEEMAN 5   GARY FARR AND THE T-BONES

YARDBIRDS

STALLS and CIRCLE : 12/6, 10/-, 7/6.
ALL SEATS MAY BE BOOKED IN ADVANCE

POSTAL BOOKING FORM

To: THE BOX OFFICE

Please forward _____ Stalls/Circle (No. of Seats) at _____ (Price)

for the _____ (Time) Performance on _____ (Date)

for which I enclose stamped addressed envelope with remittance value £ : :

NAME _____

ADDRESS _____

WHEWELL'S OF BOLTON

The flyer (above left) – with postal booking form attached – for a 1965 Marquee-promoted package tour varied its design style for each act, including, in the case of the Yardbirds, the group's own typography. The band's distinctive 'logo' was designed by Hamish Grimes, who at the time shared an office with the Yardbirds manager, Giorgio Gomelsky – who also ran the Crawdaddy Club in Richmond. When the Yardbirds succeeded the Rolling Stones as the house band at that venue in 1963, Gomelsky asked Grimes to produce a striking image to advertise his new band. Grimes duly obliged.

The 'Barbeque 67' event, despite being at the start of the 'Summer of Love', was billed conventionally – although the line-up of acts, including Jimi Hendrix, Cream and Pink Floyd, was, even then, good value at £1!

BARBEQUE 67

TULIP BULB AUCTION HALL
SPALDING, LINCS.

SPRING BANK HOLIDAY MONDAY
(NON-STOP DANCING 4 P.M. IN AFTERNOON UNTIL 12 P.M. AT NIGHT)

MAY 29

TO THE TOP SIX

JIMI HENDRIX EXPERIENCE   **CREAM**

GENO WASHINGTON AND THE RAM JAM BAND

PINK FLOYD   **MOVE**

ZOOT MONEY AND HIS BIG ROLL BAND

LICENSED BAR APPLIED FOR—HOT DOGS
DISCOTHEQUE FROM 4 P.M.— COVERED ACCOMMODATION
SOFT ULTRA VIOLET LIGHTING   KNOCKOUT ATMOSPHERE

ADMISSION PAY AT DOOR £1

OR FOR DETAILS OF ADVANCE TICKETS AND DETAILS OF
TRANSPORT SEE LOCAL PRESS, TICKETS BY POST, SEND
S.A.E. TO ROVENGA, 3 CONERY GRDNS, WHATTON, NOTTS

ALL SUPPORTED BY

SOUNDS FORCE FIVE

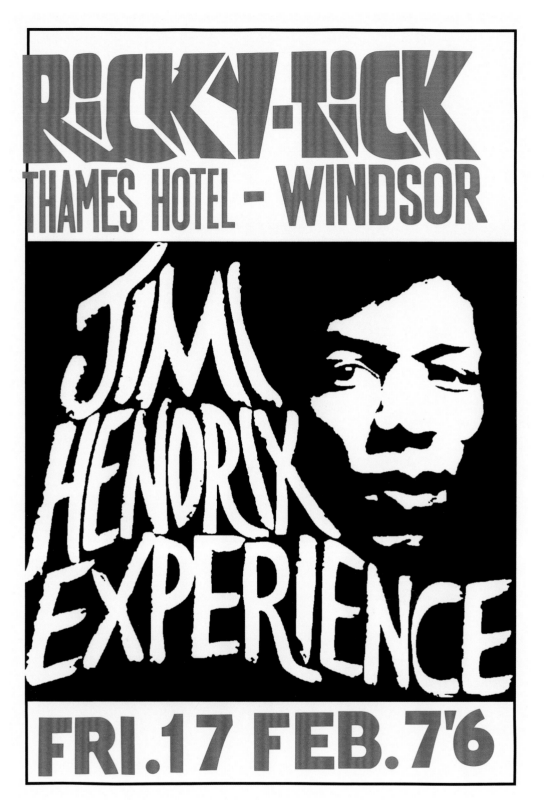

Above left
Ricky-Tick, Windsor,
February 1967

Above right
Guildhall, Southampton,
January 1967

With the influence of psychedelic graphics becoming apparent in the early months of 1967, an increasing number of individually designed posters hinted at a more fluid, 'trippy' design approach – certainly in keeping with acts like Jimi Hendrix and the Eric Clapton/Jack Bruce/Ginger Baker power trio, Cream.

Psychedelia was in full swing by the time Pink Floyd played at the All Night Garden Party – 'From 8pm till Dawn' – in Leeds in November 1967, and evidenced even more clearly in the poster for their gig at Westfield College, Hampstead, in 1968. It was a period when, with the expansion in higher education, a new circuit of potential venues developed under the auspices of individual college student unions. By the end of the decade, the social secretary of a large college could be an important booker as far as gigging bands were concerned.

Not all student posters were as in tune with psychedelic style. Despite a bill that included the Who, Arthur Brown and Jethro Tull, the poster (opposite page) for a 1967 Midnite Rave organized by Brunel University was hardly at the cutting edge of graphic design.

Above left
Queens Hall, Leeds,
November 1967

Above right
Westfield College, Hampstead,
May 1968

Right
Lyceum Ballroom, London,
October 1967

A college poster (above left) advertising the first incarnation of Fleetwood Mac, in April 1968, takes on the swirling typography of psychedelia. A key pioneer of British psychedelic design, Nigel Waymouth designed this poster (right) for the Move using the metallic fifth colours that would become a trademark of his design partnership with Michael English, and Hapshash and the Coloured Coat.

Right
Marquee Club, London
[Nigel Waymouth],
July 1967

O3

DRAW THE DREAM

THE PSYCHEDELIC EXPLOSION

Many would argue that in terms of performing its basic function – that is, to convey an instant message, advertising a particular concert or record release – the pop poster lost its way with psychedelia. Certainly, the swirling graphics and day-glo colours were often difficult to read at first glance, but that was the point: they were designed for an audience who could interpret them; a young audience schooled in the drug culture, to whom the blobby lettering and overprinting represented a very specific type of music or event.

With the emergence of large-format, four-colour lithographic printing and colour scanning, as well as improved reprographic technology, it became possible to reproduce large-scale, full-colour artworks. From the US came the airbrush – a new tool in the graphic artist's arsenal, with which photo-realistic effects could be achieved as well as near-seamless photo-retouching.

As with the music, it was a time of intense creativity. With psychedelic art, the rock poster came into its own as an object to be displayed and enjoyed for its own sake – and, as history has proved, subsequently collected and the designers lionized. Although many of the leading rock poster designers were part of the San Francisco rock scene and its immediate US offshoots, there was a strong British underground movement, led by Michael English, Nigel Waymouth, Michael McInnerney and the ex-pat Australian Martin Sharp. Other important designers included David Vaughan, John Hurford and Mal Dean, who created artworks for *International Times*.

Artists were now creating increasingly lush and colourful illustrations, harking back to the quirky styles of Aubrey Beardsley, Alphonse Mucha and Arthur Rackham, and with intricate hand-lettering to match, borrowed from the Vienna Secession. Also from America came stories of rainbow effects in underground papers and posters, which, without ever seeing them first-hand, artists like English, Waymouth and McInnerney endeavoured to recreate by experimenting with hand-printed silk-screens, and coming up with dazzling variations.

The work of such artists was typical of the movement in that it was not restricted to music-related subjects. While their posters reflected various aspects of the counterculture of the late 1960s, the artists themselves were equally involved in the broader arena of the underground press – Martin Sharp was the designer for *Oz*, for example – which would be as potent a vehicle for psychedelic style as the ubiquitous 'trippy' poster or album cover.

The 'A Is For Apple' poster (above left) was created for the Beatles by the psychedelic Dutch collective The Fool (made up of Simon Posthuma, Marijke Koger, Barry Finch and Josje Leeger) exclusively for the Beatles' Apple Boutique in London. Elements of its acid-inspired design are clearly prefigured in the swirling patterns of the Bob Dylan Albert Hall gig poster. The latter was designed by Marijke Koger when only she and Simon Posthuma were living in London – before being joined by Josje Leeger and later by her boyfriend, Englishman Barry Finch, to make The Fool. The poster was promoting Dylan's final concerts for his 1966 world tour – his first after he 'went electric'. Koger later marketed a commercial version of the *Love Dylan* poster, lacking the three lines of concert information.

Above left
Apple Boutique, London
[The Fool],
December 1967

Above right
Royal Albert Hall, London
[Marijke Koger],
May 1966

Left
Poster for Luv Me Film
Productions [Hapshash],
London, 1967

A poster (opposite) made for Luv Me Film Productions by psychedelic art pioneers Michael English and Nigel Waymouth. As the creative duo of Hapshash and the Coloured Coat, they produced a body of work that defined the ideals and visions of the time. Borrowing from the natural forms of Art Nouveau, their designs established a style that was emblematic of the flower power movement of the sixties.

Above left
UFO Club, London [Hapshash], June 1967

Above right
UFO Club, London [Hapshash], July 1967

London's short-lived but influential UFO Club, in a basement in London's Tottenham Court Road, was central to the psychedelic offerings of Hapshash and the Coloured Coat; indeed, the club was the catalyst for the duo's original collaboration. A poster for the Crazy World of Arthur Brown and Soft Machine captures the zeitgeist of a time when flying saucers were perceived as a conduit to wider spiritual understanding – as well as being great billing for the club and gig. Michael English used the level of illegibility of the poster to embody a secret message advocating another central sixties message: sexual love.

The body of the butterfly is a penis and its lower wings are spurting sperm – but the authorities never noticed or complained. The Hapshash poster for a Pink Floyd gig at the UFO Club in 1967 is a classic piece of UK psychedelia, with a phantasmagoria of castles in the air, flying saucers and swirling graphics. Michael English noted: 'All the underground posters are packed with secret signs, prehistoric forms and flying saucers . . . Sexuality, too, was a strong force and there is a lot of that happening in the posters. Dragons and pubic hair!' (The nude in this poster originally had pubic hair, but the printers insisted upon its removal.)

The Hapshash team designed posters for various occasions, most of them music-related events. The promotional poster (above left) created for Track Records in October 1967, plugging 'I Can See For Miles' by the Who, was a radical departure from the group's previous mod/pop art image. Hapshash created a whole series of posters for London's Saville Theatre, which Beatles' manager Brian Epstein had taken over in 1965; this one (above right) announces the Jimi Hendrix Experience and other acts.

The 5th Dimension club in Leicester received the Hapshash treatment in the poster (opposite) for its September 1967 line-up, which included Pink Floyd.

Above left
'I Can See For Miles' record promotion [Hapshash], October 1967

Above right
Saville Theatre, London [Hapshash], August 1967

Opposite
5th Dimension club, Leicester [Hapshash], September 1967

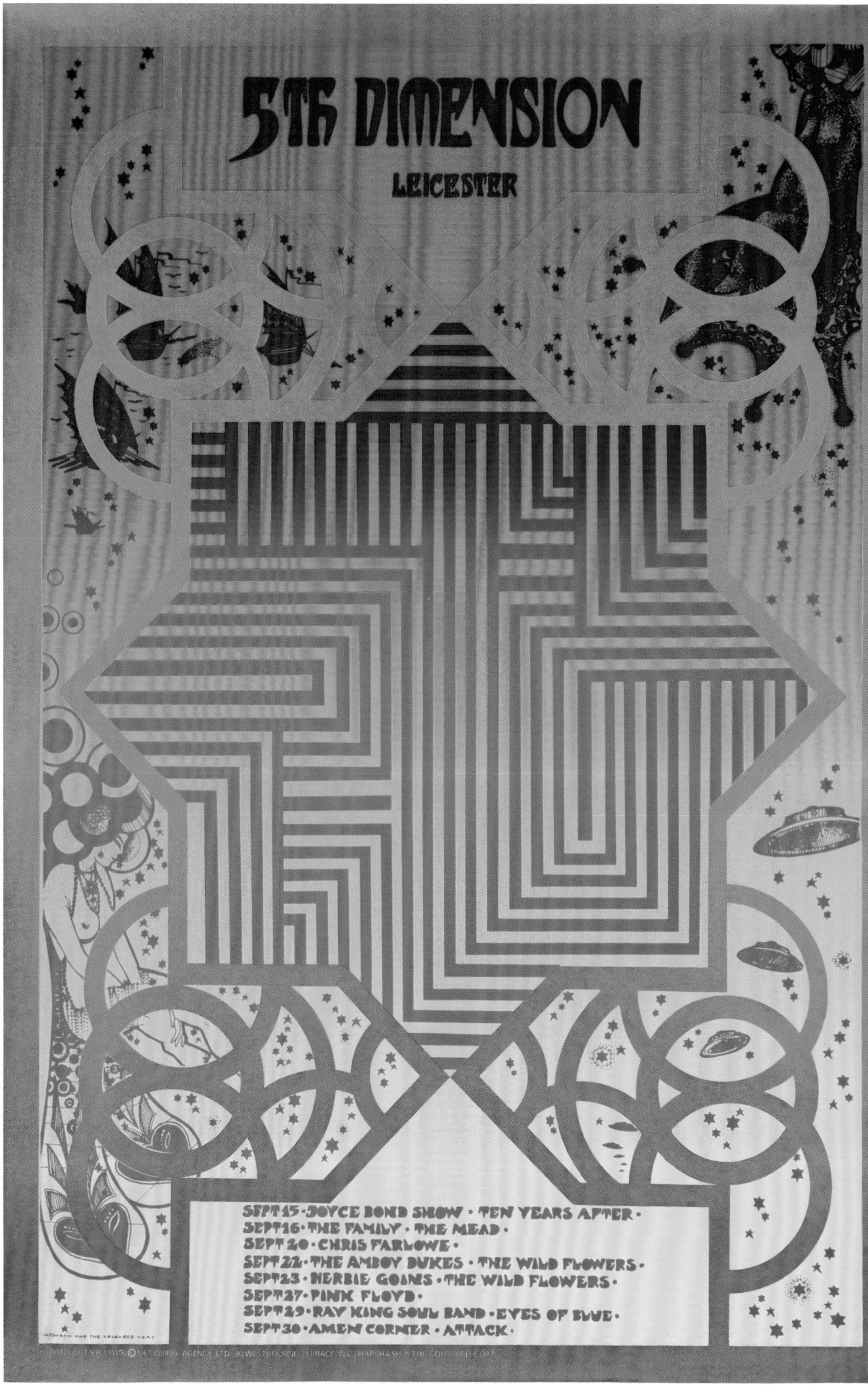

5TH DIMENSION
LEICESTER
SEPT 15 · JOYCE BOND SHOW · TEN YEARS AFTER ·
SEPT 16 · THE FAMILY · THE MEAD ·
SEPT 20 · CHRIS FARLOWE ·
SEPT 22 · THE AMBOY DUKES · THE WILD FLOWERS ·
SEPT 23 · HERBIE GOINS · THE WILD FLOWERS ·
SEPT 27 · PINK FLOYD ·
SEPT 29 · RAY KING SOUL BAND · EYES OF BLUE ·
SEPT 30 · AMEN CORNER · ATTACK ·
HAPSHASH AND THE COLOURED COAT

HAPSHASH

If one name sums up British psychedelic art of the sixties, it's that of the design team known as Hapshash and the Coloured Coat. Part of the fabric of London's 'hippy' counterculture, their posters – particularly for the underground club UFO – were instant icons in their own time, and have since become collector's items on a par with conventional works of art.

In December 1966, Nigel Waymouth and Michael English, two graphic designers, met at the Granny Takes a Trip clothes shop on the King's Road in order to discuss a collaboration; both were involved with the underground scene that was just starting up. Earlier that year, John Hopkins and Joe Boyd of the London Free School (LFS) in Notting Hill had launched a series of fundraising benefit concerts in a church hall, featuring an unknown band called the Pink Floyd. Hopkins subsequently became co-founder of *International Times*, Europe's first underground newspaper, and in this role was looking for a way to supplement his staff's meagre wages. Hopkins and Boyd decided to repeat the LFS formula in the West End, with the UFO Club. At Hopkins' request, the first UFO Club poster was designed by Michael English; Boyd also wanted his friend Waymouth to design for them – hence the meeting in the King's Road. The pair initially decided to work together as Cosmic Colours, but only produced one poster under that name; then as Jacob and the Coloured Coat, which lasted for just two posters, before settling on Hapshash and the Coloured Coat in March 1967. The name came about during an evening spent looking at books on Egyptology, and was a derivative of Queen Hatshepsut – modified to incorporate the word 'hash'.

Born in 1941, Nigel Waymouth had originally graduated in economic history before attending courses at various London art schools. Then, early in 1966, with two partners he opened the first clothes boutique in the King's Road aimed specifically at the new counterculture, calling it Granny Takes A Trip. As well as creating the interior design and psychedelic frontage of the shop, Waymouth designed many of the early clothes on sale.

Also born in 1941, Michael English had studied at Ealing School of Art and had some earlier successes during the pop art craze with t-shirts, carrier bags and sunglasses. After meeting Waymouth, he helped paint the mural of a Red Indian's head on the shop frontage of Granny Takes A Trip, as well as that of another famous boutique of the era, Hung On You.

The trademark Hapshash style encapsulated the key characteristics of psychedelic poster art, with swirling graphics, bright colours, and a strong Art Nouveau influence reminiscent of early 20th-century artists such as Alphonse Mucha and Aubrey Beardsley. It was also replete with visual references to the various elements of hippy lore, including astrology, UFOs, fairy-tale castles and the like. They were the first to perfect a technique of rainbow silk-screens, as Michael English explained: 'The artwork for each colour was transferred to its own individual screen and the elements of the image were married together in the actual process of printing. We developed our own technique of putting two or three colours onto the screen, merging them together as the squeegee was pulled across. That was our most successful innovation.' One panel might start off green and turn to yellow at the bottom of the print; another might run from gold to silver: 'We used metallic and fluorescent inks – day-glo!'

The pair's posters were printed and distributed by Joe Boyd's company Osiris Visions. Although Waymouth and English continued working for UFO, their work extended to both the *International Times* itself and, significantly, the more design-driven *Oz* magazine, plus one-off commissions that included other rock venues, counterculture events and at least one record sleeve (their own) which they pressed on red transparent plastic. *Hapshash and the Coloured Coat featuring the Human Host and the Heavy Metal Kids* was a bizarre concept album, in which Waymouth and English (neither of them singers or musicians) were backed by a band called Art while they banged tambourines and generally made a racket. Waymouth later recalled that the rhythm guitar player 'got so pissed off, he said, "This isn't rock 'n' roll!" and stormed out.'

The partnership lasted for two years as Hapshash and the Coloured Coat. But, by the end of the sixties, the original idealism of the hippy movement was starting to fade – and, along with it, that of many of its founding movers and shakers. Yet with the rich body of work produced in that relatively short period, Hapshash were guaranteed a place in the pantheon of rock poster design. In Autumn 2000, the Victoria and Albert Museum (which holds many of their key works in its permanent collection) held a large retrospective of their work, and in 2005 Hapshash posters featured heavily in the Tate Gallery Liverpool's exhibition 'Summer of Love: Psychedelic Art, 1967'.

'Our concept was to plaster the streets of London with this very brightly coloured and beautiful poster work at a time when most of the posters in the streets were rather drab and wordy. You had concert bills put up for the Marquee club or whatever, just announcing Manfred Mann in bold letters. What we tried to do was zap them, as we said, with colour and chaos to the eyes, so that people would be attracted to this blast. It was a precursor to graffiti, in a way. It's sort of between pop art and graffiti. We were trying to push the boundaries of the visual aspect of pop. We felt like we were illustrating an ideal. We were trying to give a visual concept of what we were experiencing . . . So one week we'd be doing a poster that was very heavily visually illustrative in a sort of nursery-rhyme way or a childlike way, using images from turn-of-the-century illustrators. The next week we'd be quite boldly doing almost op-art things. It was a mix of things.'

Nigel Waymouth

Right
The Crazy World of Arthur
Brown promotional poster
[Hapshash],
1967

The Hapshash poster (opposite) for Jimi Hendrix at San Francisco's famed Fillmore Auditorium was not, in fact, an official Fillmore poster; apparently, Hendrix commissioned the piece himself. *Love, Love, Love: The New Love Poetry* was a 1967 book of poetry edited by Pete Roche, for which Hapshash designed the cover; they also created the Julie Felix Royal Albert Hall poster from 1968.

Above left
Love Love Love: The New Love Poetry book cover [Hapshash], October 1967

Above right
Royal Albert Hall, London [Hapshash], April 1968

Above left
Portrait of Ringo Starr
[Alan Aldridge],
1969

Above right
Portrait of George Harrison
[Alan Aldridge],
1969

Illustrator (or 'graphic entertainer', as he has dubbed himself) Alan Aldridge produced numerous pictures of the Beatles, with imagery often inspired by the group's song titles or themes. Such images include selected illustrations in *The Beatles Illustrated Lyrics*, which Aldridge compiled and edited, and was first published in 1969. The Lennon image from this title, shown above right, illustrated the song 'There's A Place' – first released on the Beatles' debut album *Please Please Me*. The image of Ringo (opposite, above left) as the face of the Yellow Submarine is from the same publication, as is the portrait of George performing 'My Guitar Gently Weeps' (opposite, above right). 'Paul as Sgt. Pepper' was produced to accompany an article by Aldridge entitled 'The Beatles' Sinister Songbook', which was the fruit of a three-hour interview with McCartney.

Above left
Paul McCartney [Alan Aldridge],
1969

Above right
John Lennon [Alan Aldridge],
1969

UNDERGROUND PRESS

The psychedelic style that characterized rock posters in the late 1960s was not restricted to the music scene. It was nurtured and given its broadest canvas in the underground press – the network of alternative newspapers and magazines that was a central focus of the 'hippy' counterculture.

The earliest, and arguably most influential, UK underground paper was the *International Times*, which soon after its first issue had to change its name to *IT* following threats of legal action from *The Times* newspaper. *IT* was founded in London in 1966 by John Hopkins, Barry Miles and others, with financial assistance from Paul McCartney, and its close links with the emerging alternative music scene were apparent from the start. The broadsheet-style paper was launched on October 15, 1966 at an 'All Night Rave' at the Roundhouse, which featured up-and-coming psychedelic bands Soft Machine and Pink Floyd. Among the fancy-dressed audience was Marianne Faithful, dressed as a nun, and Paul McCartney in Middle Eastern garb. It was one of the first times that a light show had been used by a UK rock band, as the *Sunday Times* reported: 'At the launching of the new magazine *IT* the other night a pop group called the Pink Floyd played throbbing music, while a series of bizarre coloured shapes flashed on a huge screen behind them.' The event was later described by Soft Machine's guitarist Daevid Allen as 'One of the two most revolutionary events in the history of English alternative music and thinking.' He went on: 'The *IT* event was important because it marked the first recognition of a rapidly spreading socio-cultural revolution that had its parallel in the States.'

In many ways, *IT* pioneered what would become conventional graphic styles in underground publishing,

artwork for offset lithography, which gave more freedom in the layout of pages and use of images. The paper's logo was a black and white image of the silent film star Theda Bara – they had planned to use an image of Clara Bow, as she'd been known as the 'It Girl', but the Bara picture was used by mistake.

Like many other magazines and newspapers of the underground press, *IT* was hounded by the police. In April 1967, when police raids were threatening to force it out of business, the paper staged a now-legendary 'free speech' fundraising benefit. Called the '14 Hour Technicolor Dream', the event heralded the 'Summer of Love', and was one of the biggest gatherings of the flower power era. The spectacular poster by Michael McInnerney advertised a huge line-up that included Pink Floyd, Soft Machine, the Velvet Underground, Frank Zappa, the Who, John Lennon and Yoko Ono.

Alongside *IT*, the other ground-breaking underground publication was *Oz*, which made an even bigger impact in terms of its illustrative content. Originally an Australian magazine, the British version was launched when its founders Richard Neville and artist Martin Sharp moved to London. With fellow Australian Jim Anderson they launched a visually stunning paper, put together using new production techniques that included metallic foil, fluorescent inks and offset printing. This gave Sharp, the Hapshash team and other designers an opportunity for psychedelic magazine illustration that has never been matched since.

Underground magazines proliferated during the late 1960s, each with its own visual style, from the Tolkien-inspired *Gandalf's Garden* to the provocative comic-book satire of *Nasty Tales*. And while the hippy dreamers drifted off into a hallucinogenic world of their own, the political edge of the counterculture came to the fore during the student unrest of 1968.

ALL NIGHT RAVE to launch new underground newspaper 'INTERNATIONAL TIMES' the Soft Machine; the Pink Floyd; Steel Bands

STRIP – TRIPS – HAPPENING
MOVIE – POP – OP – COSTUME
MASQUE – DRAG BALL

bring your own poison, bring Flowers & Gass filled balloons SUrPRIZE for Shortest & Barest at...

THE ROUND HOUSE ✳
OPP. chalk farm underground

SAT. 15th OCT 11 P.M. onwards

advance tickets 5'- from INDICA better books; Dobells Record Shop.

GRANNIE TAKE A TRIP Mandarin Book Shops at ... Nottinghill gate & Swiss cottage, or compulsory donations of 10'- at door.

Right
Poster announcing the first
edition of Oz magazine
[Martin Sharp],
February 1967

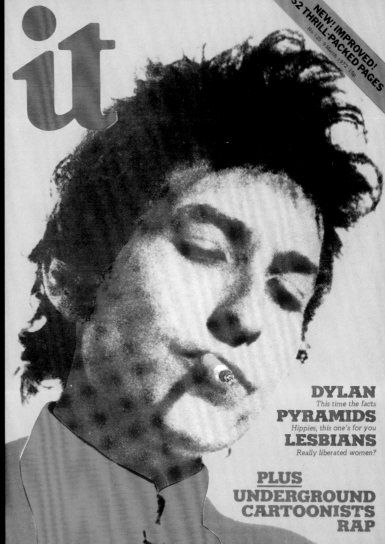

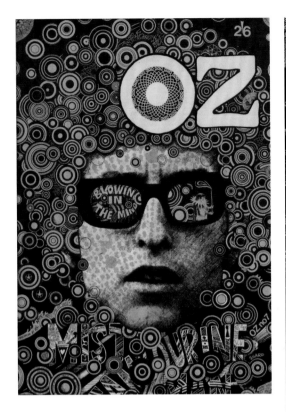

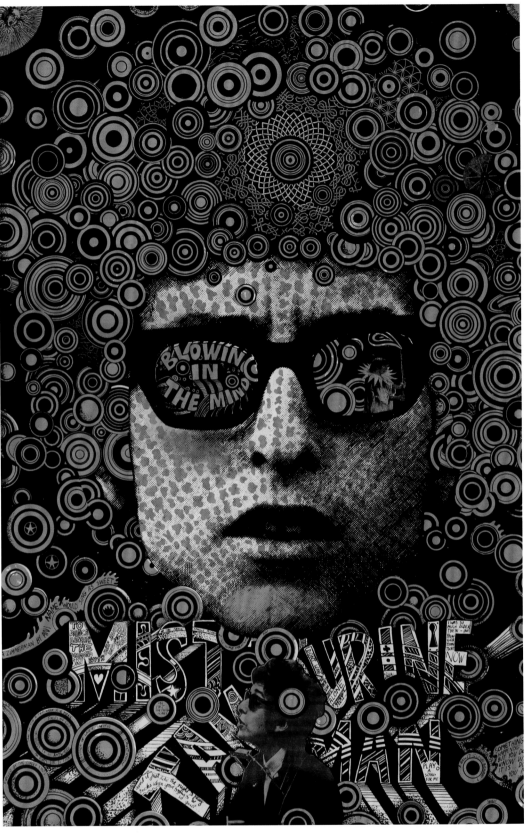

One of the co-founders of the original *Oz* magazine in Australia, and art director and leading cartoonist of the more celebrated UK version, Martin Sharp is regarded as one of the leading designers of the psychedelic era. His 'Blowing In The Mind' portrait of 'Mr Tambourine Man' Bob Dylan became a hugely familiar poster, having started life as the cover of *Oz* magazine's 7th edition.

Above left
Oz #7 cover [Martin Sharp],
October 1967

Above right
'Blowing In The Mind' poster
[Martin Sharp],
1967

Sharp spearheaded the design
innovations that *Oz* quickly became
famous for, such as his huge collage
poster 'Plant A Flower Child' (above),
made from photographs of identical
twins Nicole and Michelle from Toronto.
Photographed by Bob Whitaker, and
issued as *Oz* magazine #5 in July
1967, it was described as a 'special
surprise issue!' This is the yellow first
printing; the second was in pink. In the
music world, Sharp was also famous
for album covers for the band Cream,
which inspired spin-off posters such
as the one shown on the left.

Above left
Cream poster [Martin Sharp],
November 1967

Above right
'Plant A Flower Child' poster
[Martin Sharp],
July 1969

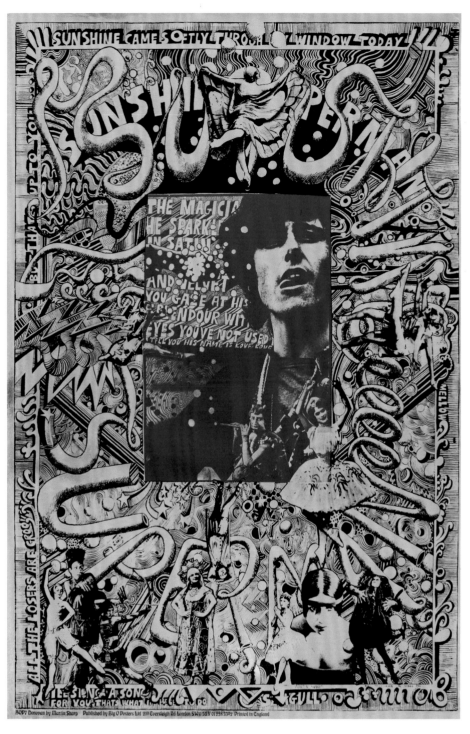

Left
'Live Give Love' poster
[Martin Sharp],
1967

Above
'Sunshine Superman' poster
[Martin Sharp],
1967

Both created on a metallic silver background, 'Live Give Love' and the Donovan 'Sunshine Superman' poster are typical of some of the technical extremes that were being explored in Martin Sharp's work during the late sixties. Intertwined with images of ballerinas and the like, the artwork of folk-rock singer Donovan (above) was surrounded by snippets from the lyrics of his songs.

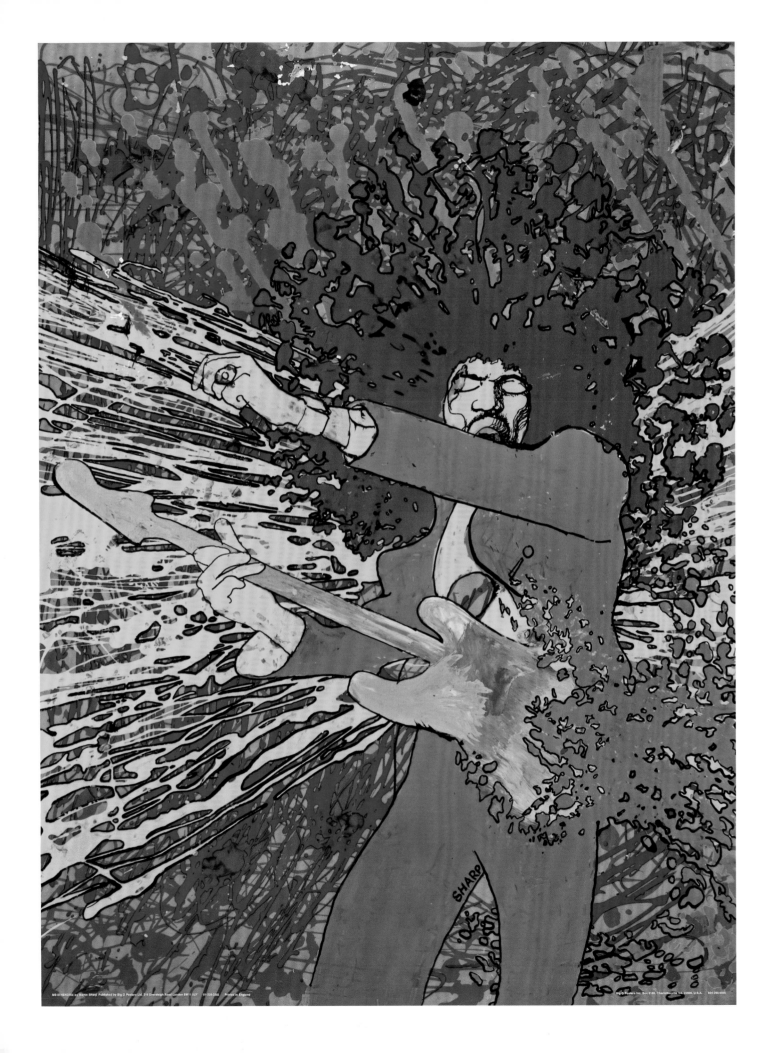

Martin Sharp's 'Exploding Hendrix' poster (opposite) has achieved iconic status over the years as the best example of the London Psychedelic School. Sharp also designed a spectacular 'Gathering of the Tribes' poster for a Legalize Pot Rally in London's Hyde Park in July 1967 (above left). Michael McInnerney, whose work was published by the Hapshash outlet Osiris, also designed an official poster for the rally using the Hapshash rainbow technique.

Opposite
'Exploding Hendrix' poster [Martin Sharp], 1967

Above left
'Gathering of the Tribes', Hyde Park, London [Martin Sharp], July 1967

Above right
Legalize Pot Rally, Hyde Park, London [Michael McInnerney], July 1967

alexis korner
alex harvey
creation
charlie brown's
clowns
champion jack
dupree
denny laine
gary farr
graham bond
ginger johnson
jacob's ladder
construction co.
move
one one seven
pink floyd
poetry band
purple gang
pretty things
pete townshend
pajson bellows
soft machine
sun trolley
social deviants
stalkers
the utterly incredible
too long ago
to remember
sometimes shouting
at people
marc sullivan
martin doughty
maureen pape
john pape
mike stocks
noel murphy
dave russell
christopher logue
barry fantoni
ron geeson
john fahey
the velvet underground
the who
frank zappa and the
mothers of invention
john lennon
yoko ono
marc bolan
the flies
tomorrow

international times
free speech benefit
alexandra palace N.22
8pm saturday
29 april–sun 30
tickets £1
in advance–only

indica better books collets
dobells dave curtis 57 greek
st w.1 ger 1548 and main
it distributors
or your local agent
bus shuttle from wood green
highgate 8.12pm

Above left
'Buy Granny Takes a Trip and
Join the Brain Drain'
[Hapshash],
1968

Above right
The Roundhouse, London
[Michael McInnerney],
April 1967

Michael McInnerney was responsible
for the poster for the now-legendary
14 Hour Technicolor Dream event at
London's Roundhouse, held to raise
legal funds for *International Times*.
Every copy of the poster was different,
as he used the rainbow printing
technique to its full advantage. Thus,
the posters vary from green to yellow
through to orange and purple, as in
the example shown above.

Nigel Waymouth, one half of the
Hapshash team, was also proprietor of
the King's Road boutique Granny Takes
A Trip; this promotional item (above
left) for the store dates from 1968.

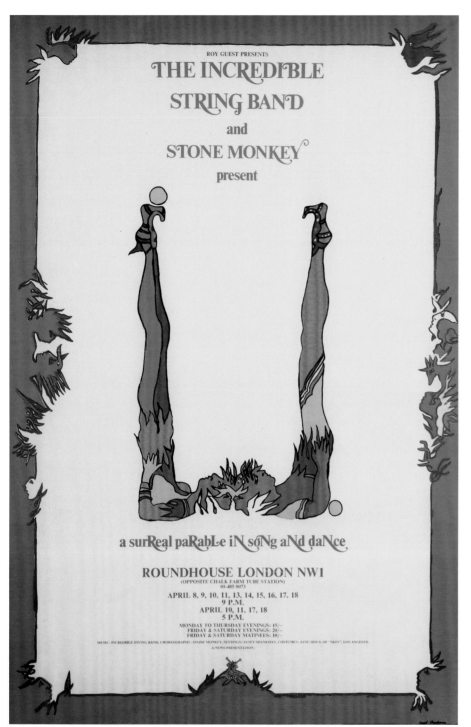

American Greg Irons had worked on the San Francisco poster scene before moving to the UK. In London, he was commissioned by Joe Boyd to create the poster (above right) advertising the folk-rock band Fairport Convention; the artwork was for Boyd's poster company Osiris, which was also a distributor of the Hapshash posters. In addition to his Osiris interests, Boyd was manager of Fairport Convention, as well as Pink Floyd and the psychedelic folk group the Incredible String Band, among others. Irons also worked on the Beatles' animated movie *Yellow Submarine*.

Janet Shankman, who later married Robin Williamson of the Incredible String Band, designed the poster above left when the ISB staged their 'Extreme Parable in Song and Dance' at the Roundhouse in north London.

Above left
The Roundhouse, London
[Janet Shankman],
April 1970

Above right
Fairport Convention promotional
poster [Greg Irons],
December 1967

One of a handful of 'psychedelic' films from the era was *Wonderwall*, which was directed by Joe Massot and featured a soundtrack by George Harrison along with sets designed by The Fool. Better known, and certainly far bigger at the box office, was the Beatles' *Yellow Submarine* from the same year of 1968 – the animated graphics of which, overseen by art director Heinz Edelmann, became part of the group's iconography in the latter part of their career.

Top
Wonderwall poster,
May 1968

Left
Yellow Submarine poster,
June 1968

Above left
Isle of Wight Festival
[Dave Roe],
August 1970

Above right
Summer of Love 40th
Anniversary, Golden Gate Park,
San Francisco [Mongsterr],
September 2007

The Isle of Wight Festival, which was inaugurated in the summer of 1968, was the major UK gathering of the psychedelic years. The artwork, from tickets and press ads to spectacular posters, was mainly the work of graphic artist Dave Roe, who created the impressive 1970 poster shown above left. Four decades later, and San Francisco celebrated the hippy ideal with a Summer of Love anniversary event – the poster, above right, being designed by the Brighton-based UK artist Jamie McGregor (a.k.a. Mongsterr).

01

PROG ROCK, ROCK, GLAM ROCK

HEADY VISTAS

Progressive rock became a powerful driving force in popular music during the 1970s, spawning a plethora of bands that enjoyed worldwide success. Amidst this creative maelstrom, all aspects of rock art flourished.

As groups such as Yes, Emerson, Lake & Palmer, Jethro Tull and Pink Floyd released a stream of 'concept' albums and embarked on stadium rock tours, so they demanded higher standards of artwork, packaging and presentation. Such expectations launched a golden age for designers, photographers, painters and art studios, who benefited from increased work opportunities and a chance to experiment with new advances in technology.

Typography and graphic art now diverged, becoming separate specialist fields and, in turn, fresh skills were required. For example, in the process known as 'headline typesetting', the setting was achieved through photosetting, whereby individual letters were exposed from a master font film, letter by letter. It was an expensive business, and was generally only applied to two or three words.

The range and size of available fonts expanded from a handful to thousands, while graphic artists, now freed from creating their own fonts, built a new industry. As a result, typography became less integrated within the final artworks, with the 'art' (itself enhanced by increasingly accomplished technical innovations such as photo-retouching) and the type often being produced by separate people. New companies sprang up that specialized exclusively in music advertising and promotion. Now teams of artworkers, rather than a single designer, would 'paste up' multi-layered black and white artworks, which were assembled using PMT (Photo Mechanical Transfer) prints, and then marked up with colour instructions for the printer on tracing paper overlays. Typically, seventies' album art credits would include an art director, a designer, a photographer, a lettering artist and a retoucher, with the retoucher becoming all-important.

Certain bands became so closely associated with their album covers that their packaging was as familiar to their fans as their music, while some of the designers, including Roger Dean, Storm Thorgerson, Paul Whitehead and Barney Bubbles, became celebrities in their own right. Predictably, much of the 'mega band' poster art of the early seventies was driven by the album cover art – and by the style leaders of the stadium rock, prog and glam music that dominated the period: David Bowie and Bryan Ferry/Roxy Music, for example. Such artists were acutely conscious of their public image. Some stunning and sometimes controversial artworks achieved iconic status on album covers, and in poster form they decorated the bedroom walls of thousands of fans.

Early artwork for progressive rock bands was an often simple affair compared with the spectacular imagery that would come to be associated with the genre. This Yes poster (right) prominently featured the band's logo, which was designed by Haig Adishian, and appeared on their debut album, *Yes*. The smaller logo in the top-left corner of the poster is for the film production company Hemdale, which in its early days (when it also functioned as a talent agency) for a time managed both Yes and Black Sabbath.

The silk-screen poster on silver-foil paper for King Crimson (above) was the work of Barry Godber, who also created the cover for the group's debut album *In the Court of the Crimson King*. The band's lyricist, Pete Sinfield, screen-printed each poster by hand.

Above left
King Crimson poster
[Barry Godber],
1969

Above right
Yes poster
[Haig Adishian],
1971

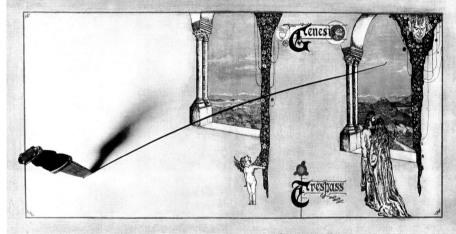

Considered by purist Genesis fans to be from the band's classic period (before singer Peter Gabriel departed to be replaced by drummer-turned-vocalist Phil Collins), the albums here appeared when the ex-Charterhouse boys were still writing lyrics infused with fantasy and mythology, rather than real-life concerns of love and relationships. Paul Whitehead's surreal artwork style seemed perfect for Genesis, and he was chosen by Peter Gabriel to provide cover artwork for their upcoming album, *Trespass*. After Whitehead heard the violent Genesis track 'The Knife', he brought out an actual knife and slashed the *Trespass* canvass, utilizing the knife as a new element in his artwork.

Top
Genesis *Nursery Cryme* album cover [Paul Whitehead], November 1971

Above right
Genesis *Trespass* album cover [Paul Whitehead], October 1970

Below right
Genesis *Foxtrot* album cover [Paul Whitehead], October 1972

Top left
Jethro Tull blank tour poster, 1968

Below left
Guildhall, Southampton, October 1970

Above right
Van der Graaf Generator promotional poster [Paul Whitehead], October 1971

Paul Whitehead's bizarre landscapes and surrealistic visualizations (exhibited in the poster above right) seemed strangely appropriate to the musical ambitions of progressive bands like Genesis and Van der Graaf Generator. Whitehead went on to design covers for the bands Renaissance, Peter Hammill and Mott the Hoople, among many others. He also designed the archetypal 'Famous Charisma Label' of the Mad Hatter. Many tour promoters, like the Chrysalis agency responsible for the Jethro Tull items shown here, would produce blank 'write-in' posters in which individual concert promoters would print or hand-write details of the gig themselves.

Above
Van der Graaf Generator
Pawn Hearts album cover
[Paul Whitehead],
October 1971

HIPGNOSIS

Formed in 1968, graphic art team Hipgnosis were hugely influential in British rock illustration. Most of their work was in the field of album covers, particularly for Pink Floyd, although they created a variety of memorable sleeves for other bands through the 1970s, including Genesis, Led Zeppelin and Black Sabbath. Their style was to impact on rock 'n' roll visuals through the seventies and beyond.

The design team was formed by Storm Thorgerson, who at the time was a roommate of Floyd's Syd Barrett. Thorgerson had done some covers for pulp cowboy novels with Aubrey 'Po' Powell, and the band asked them if they could come up with something 'spacey and psychedelic' for their second album, *Saucerful of Secrets*. It transpired that Pink Floyd were only the second band, after the Beatles, that EMI Records allowed to use an outside designer for their album cover. With 13 separate images superimposed on one another, it was one of the first truly psychedelic sleeves to appear in the UK; but it was with their later work for Floyd that Thorgerson and Powell (with a third partner, Peter Christopherson) made their mark as Hipgnosis. Their attention-grabbing covers, though often starkly simple, set a benchmark for rock art in the era of 'progressive' music.

Ummagumma, released in 1969, had Pink Floyd posing by a picture of the band, posing by a picture of the band, and so on ad infinitum, while *Atom Heart Mother* the following year had just a cow in a field looking around at the camera. But there was something almost surreal about the image of the solitary animal. It was a mood to be repeated in much of the later Hipgnosis work with the band, including *Wish You Were Here* (1975) with its men shaking hands, one in flames, and 1977's memorable *Animals* with the inflatable pink pig flying over London's Battersea Power Station.

Now considered one of the most recognizable album covers of all time, *Dark Side of the Moon* (1973) was simplicity itself, showing just the (albeit carefully crafted) image of a shaft of white light being transformed into a rainbow via a prism.

Though their designs suggest otherwise, none of Hipgnosis' or Thorgerson's later work was created with the aid of computers. Everything was shot 'naturally' (even if some items were photographed separately and then put together), as Thorgerson explained in an interview in 1997 with the Floydian Slip fan website: 'If we arranged some kind of . . . set or some kind of grouping of people or some kind of event, or some kind of sculpture or installation, we would set it up and shoot it. We might shoot it in bits, but it would all be shot for real. And that, I think, is because in some ineffable fashion, it's always better. Obviously you can do all sorts of things in a computer that look better for doing them in a computer, but they are computer things.'

As well as creating no fewer than ten covers for Pink Floyd, Hipgnosis also worked for scores of other prominent bands. Among the well-remembered covers they produced were designs for T-Rex (*Electric Warrior*), Wishbone Ash (*Argus*), Led Zeppelin's *Houses of the Holy*, the desert landscape of The Nice's *Elegy*, 10cc's *Original Soundtrack* and *Venus and Mars* by Wings. The surreal approach of Thorgerson and co. was never bettered than in the weirdly normal setting of UFO's *Phenomenon* in 1974, which featured a flying saucer hovering over the red-roofed bungalow and neat lawn of suburbia in the fifties, and the disturbing sexuality of 1979's *Lovedrive* by the Scorpions, which earned the accolade of 'Best album sleeve of 1979' from *Playboy* magazine, followed by a change of cover for the American release. Hipgnosis became a design group in 1983, but in their time were responsible for some of the most enduring images of British rock music.

'Hipgnosis . . . jettisoned album cover art out of the usual fare of band mugshots to something far more epic. Their work has influenced design and advertising ever since.'
Andy Polaine, editor, *The Designer's Review of Books*, 2008 (www.designersreviewofbooks.com)

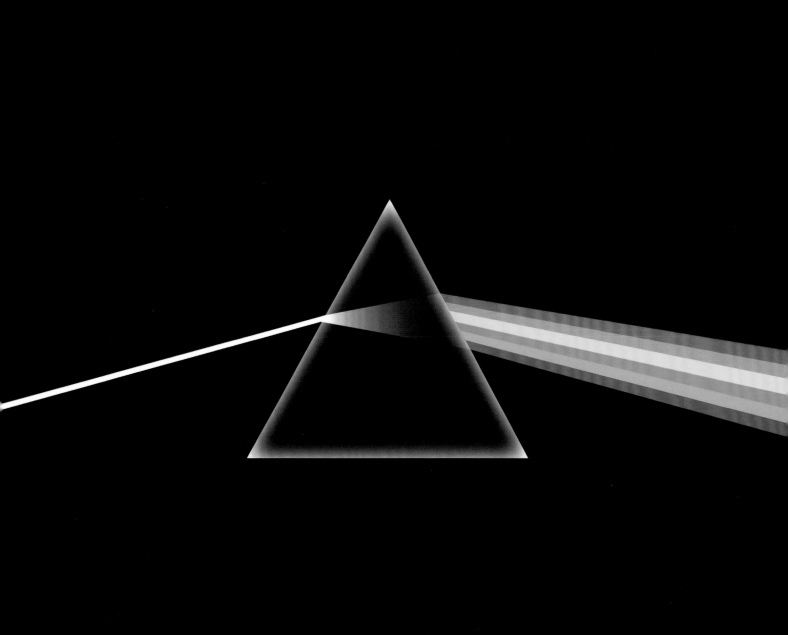

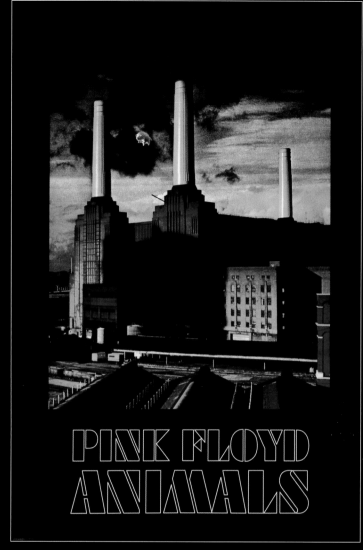

Above left
Pink Floyd *Pulse* promotional
poster [Hipgnosis],
May 1995

Above right
Pink Floyd *Animals* promotional
poster [Hipgnosis],
January 1977

Below right
Pink Floyd *Atom Heart Mother*
promotional poster [Hipgnosis],
October 1970

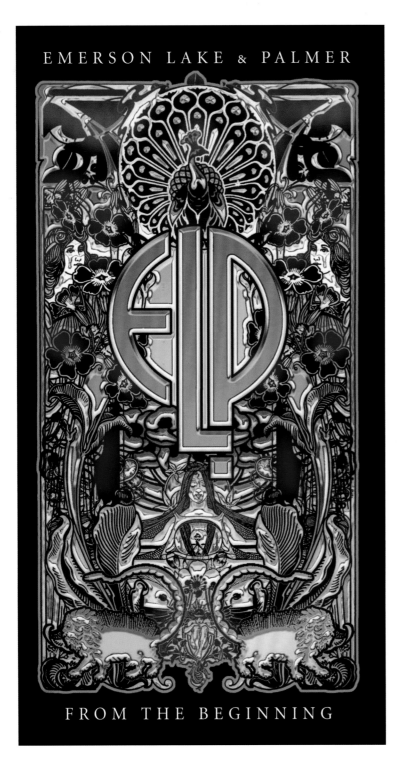

Alongside vintage items dating from a band's early career, there is now a thriving collectable market for artwork created in more recent times. Such collectable items often draw inspiration from the art of those early days, although the examples shown here are more illustrative of an earlier psychedelic era. This ELP box set (above left) from 2007 was designed by Hugh Gilmour and incorporates the group's official logo, while the poster for Yes at the Rainbow Theatre during their 1972 'Fragile' tour, shown opposite, was produced as a commemorative poster over 30 years after the event.

Above left
Emerson, Lake & Palmer
From The Beginning box set
cover [Hugh Gilmour],
2007

Above right
Emerson, Lake & Palmer
European Tour poster,
April–May 1974

Above left
Yes at the Rainbow Theatre,
commemorative poster
[Steve Harradine],
January 2003

Above right
City Hall, Sheffield,
October 1971

ROGER DEAN

What Roger Dean describes as 'fantastical' landscapes epitomized the progressive rock album covers – and their spin-off posters – of the 1970s; they continue to resonate today as classics of the genre. Dean's work was as integral to prog rock art as that of Storm Thorgerson and Hipgnosis.

Born in Ashford, Kent, in 1944, Dean attended Canterbury College of Art, where he obtained a Diploma in Design before gaining a place on a furniture design course at the Royal College of Art in London. And, unlikely though it might seem, it was through a furniture project that Dean first became involved in rock music illustration.

Dean explains: 'When I was in my second year at the Royal College, I had a piece of furniture on exhibition at the Design Centre called the Sea Urchin Chair, which attracted the attention of various furniture manufacturers. One was Form International, whose MD Monty Berman asked me if I'd design some furniture for them. The first project which he gave me was the seating for the discotheque at Ronnie Scott's jazz club. It was like a landscape, a foam seating landscape you could walk up, like a hill of foam, but wherever you sat you had a proper lumber support. It was comfortable to sit on, and it looked very exotic.' Scott and the club's co-manager Pete King loved the furniture, and when Dean showed them his sketchbook they asked if they could use a particular painting for an album cover. Dean adds, 'that was my first album cover, for the group Gun, and that was in 1968.'

More record cover work followed, though at first it did not fully exploit Dean's talent for the fantastic. 'Gun was signed to CBS,' explains Dean, 'and the head of A&R there at the time was a man called David Howells . . . he was a big supporter of my work, but Ronnie Scott was signed for his jazz music to the Vertigo label, so they asked me to do a whole series of jazz covers. But Vertigo wanted something very austere in design, and I wanted to do something a lot more fantastical, more flamboyant, like I did for Gun.'

When Howells moved to MCA Records, he contacted Dean and gave him the job of working on the first album cover for the Afro-rock band Osibisa, which turned out to be a bigger success than anyone had anticipated, and not just as an album cover. Recalls Dean, 'It also allowed me to get a poster contract with Big O posters, and we sold hundreds of thousands; it was a very interesting period for me, both in terms of my reputation and financially, because the posters really did sell very well.'

Big O was run by Peter Ledeboer, who had been art director of Oz magazine and so was steeped in the world of psychedelia; Ledeboer was initially unconvinced about Dean's illustrations, as Dean admits: 'Peter's first posters were by Martin Sharp, who did the covers for the band Cream, and his posters were absolutely psychedelic. I didn't think mine were; mine were definitely a change in direction from the psychedelic stuff. To be honest, Peter was a bit unsure of my work when I showed it to him, but his head of sales at the time, a man called Ron Ford, insisted they got done, and in the end we sold millions.'

Eagerly seeking work, Dean met up with the band with whom his work has been most closely associated, Yes. 'I would take my portfolio around the various record companies and band managements, and then I saw Phil Carson at Atlantic, and he said "I'd love to give you a job, but I only have two bands," and that was Led Zeppelin and Yes . . . and he said he'd give me a call when one of them needed a cover. He didn't give me the job, but he made an introduction, and I had to sell myself to the band . . . but that worked out fine.'

Roger Dean's imagery seemed to chime with the mood of progressive rock in a way that other styles simply would not have done, although he insists that his particular artwork style was not entirely unique in that respect: 'You could say the same about Storm's stuff – and King Crimson's *In The Court of the Crimson King*, that was a brilliant cover . . . yes, I was lucky. I'd never heard the term "prog rock" until many years after, and wasn't really aware that there was any such thing at the time.'

'With Yes . . . it didn't really seem appropriate to sell the music on the basis of the look of the band; they wanted to push it to another place, and that's what we did.'
Roger Dean, 2010

Opposite, top
Yes logo [Roger Dean], 1972

Opposite, below
Virgin Records label logo [Roger Dean], 1972

2001 NEARFEST

ANDERSON BRUFORD
WAKEMAN HOWE

ON COMPACT DISC · ALBUM · CASSETTE

ARISTA

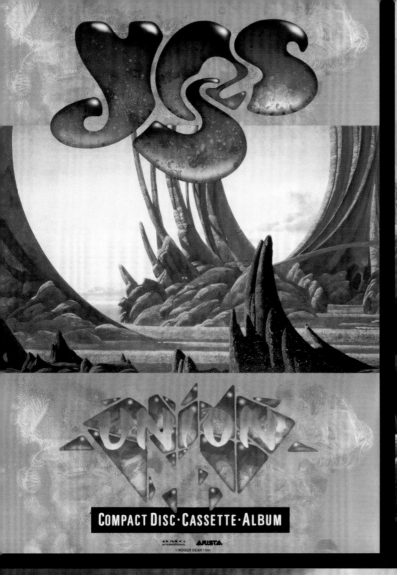

UNION

COMPACT DISC · CASSETTE · ALBUM

BMG INTERNATIONAL   ARISTA
© ROGER DEAN 1991

Greenslade

THEIR NEW ALBUM OUT NOW

Available on Atla

Above
Steve Howe *Beginnings*
promotional poster
[Roger Dean],
October 1975

92 __ THE ART OF BRITISH ROCK

Howe
nings

records and tapes.

Steve Howe Beginnings Posters Atlantic Atco © 1975

Although they were not from the same stable as the other progressive rock bands of the day, 1970s 'space rockers' Hawkwind were associated with artworks that were definitely rooted in the prog rock style. Their artist was Barney Bubbles, who later in the decade would be a major name in new wave design, helping to create visual identities for acts including Elvis Costello and Ian Dury. In the posters featured on this page, Bubbles was still very much appropriating retro imagery, from the Alphonse Mucha-influenced 'Love & Peace' poster (based on the *Champagne White Star* artwork for Moët & Chandon in 1899), via the art deco/Cassandre-inspired style of *Roadhawks*, to the tongue-in-cheek fascist triumphalism of 1976's *Astounding Sounds, Amazing Music.*

Above left
Hawkwind 'Love & Peace'
poster [Barney Bubbles],
1974

Above right
Hawkwind *Roadhawks*
promotional poster
[Barney Bubbles],
April 1976

Below right
Hawkwind letterhead
[Barney Bubbles],
1972

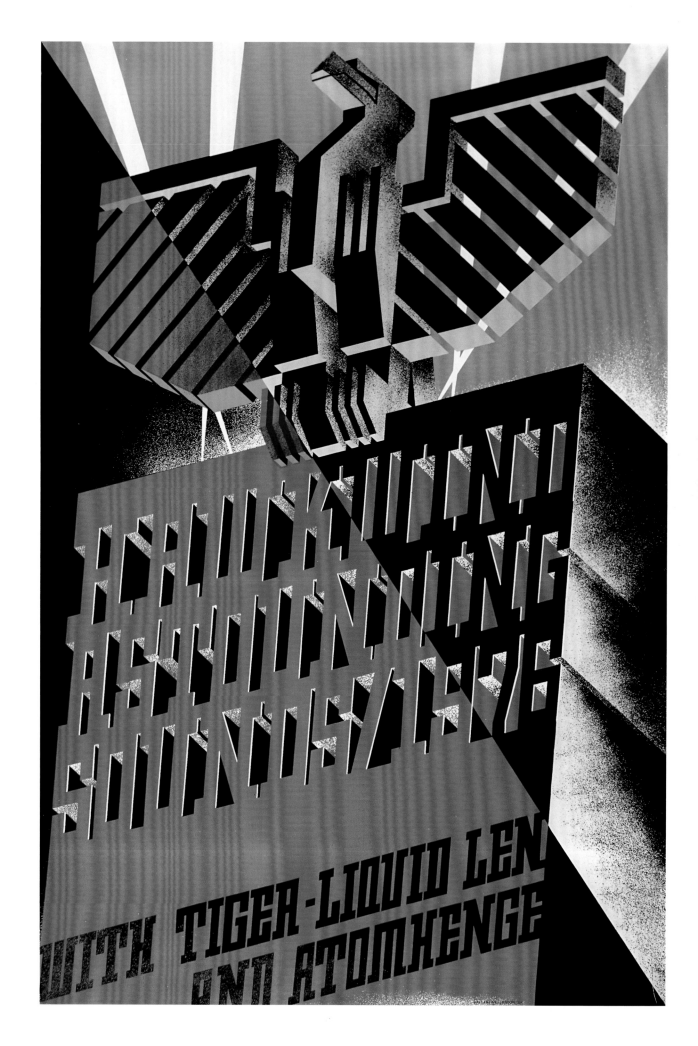

Right
Hawkwind *Astounding Sounds* promotional poster [Barney Bubbles], August 1976

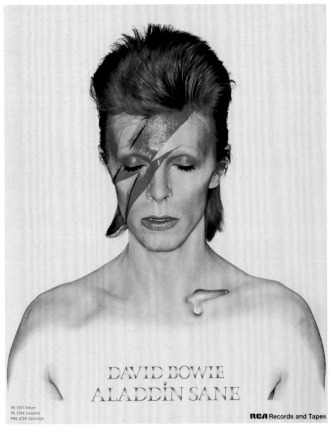

In glam rock design more emphasis was put on the individual look and appeal of the performers than on surrealistic imagery. This was especially true of David Bowie during his Ziggy period. Photographer Brian Duffy and his design company created the above cover for *Aladdin Sane*, so named because Duffy misheard Bowie saying 'A Lad Insane'. Duffy pinched the 'flash' symbol from a logo on a National Panasonic rice cooker he had in the studio, which was applied to Bowie's face using red lipstick. Philip Castle was then brought in to airbrush directly onto the only Dye Transfer Colour print produced. All *Aladdin Sane* reproductions came from this master copy, which is now stored safely in a bank vault. Above left is the original George Underwood cartoon poster that was created to promote the Ziggy Stardust album.

Above left
David Bowie *Ziggy Stardust* promotional poster
[George Underwood],
1972

Above right
David Bowie *Aladdin Sane* album poster
[Brian Duffy],
1973

Supercharge
HORIZONTAL REFRESHMENT

Above
Supercharge *Horizontal Refreshment* cover
[Photography: Clive Arrowsmith],
1977

Sheer sex appeal was another vital and challenging feature of 1970s album art. It was the era of 'Page Three Girls' in the tabloid press and sexy images in posters were a big hit with mainly male rock fans. Roxy Music used several high-profile models for their covers, including *Playboy* Playmate of the Year Marilyn Coles (on *Stranded*) and Jerry Hall on *For Your Pleasure* and *Siren*. The scantily clad girls on *Country Life* (Constanze Karoli and Eveline Grunwald) were lesser known; Bryan Ferry had met the two German fans while relaxing in Portugal, and persuaded them to do the shoot. The model for the debut album by Nutz was Linda Halpin, wife of the renowned designer Geoff Halpin who also designed the cover.

Above left
Nutz promotional poster
[Geoff Halpin],
1974

Above right
Roxy Music *Country Life*
promotional poster
[Bryan Ferry/Nick de Ville],
November 1974

Below right
Roxy Music *Siren*
promotional poster
[Bryan Ferry/Nick de Ville],
October 1975

05

PUNK &NEW WAVE

THE ART OF DO-IT-YOURSELF

When punk exploded onto the UK rock scene in 1976, it was in reaction to the increasingly corporate world of record company promotion, mainstream concerts and the pretentiousness of so-called 'progressive' rock. This attitude was reflected in punk's graphic material, which forged a brand-new, anti-establishment aesthetic. The punk ethos was one of 'do-it-yourself' – many bands revelled in the fact that they could barely play their instruments – and this extended to the scene's 'home-made' gig posters and fanzines.

Punk design consciously avoided anything slick and glossy, and instead favoured naive techniques and 'street-cred' authenticity; posters and album covers were deliberately created to look poorly drawn – cut-up, thrown together and cheaply reproduced. This new style, pioneered by artists like Jamie Reid in his work with the Sex Pistols, was soon being adopted by a fresh generation of art school graduates. Despite his apparently unschooled approach, Reid drew on a variety of fine art influences, from Constructivism and Dadaist cut-ups to political propaganda posters. Other influences – in the clean-cut, Bauhaus-inspired designs of Malcolm Garrett, for example – were also appropriated in the cause of the new music.

With the new wave bands that followed in the wake of punk, independent record companies sprang up. These labels were freed from the constraints of the established companies, and so provided a perfect creative environment for the new breed of image makers. Although the leading record majors would quickly catch on, often clumsily imitating the punk trailblazers, the new 'indies', such as Stiff, Rough Trade and 2-Tone – all with highly individual label styles – would produce memorable images that came to define not just the music, but also the era of which it was inextricably a part.

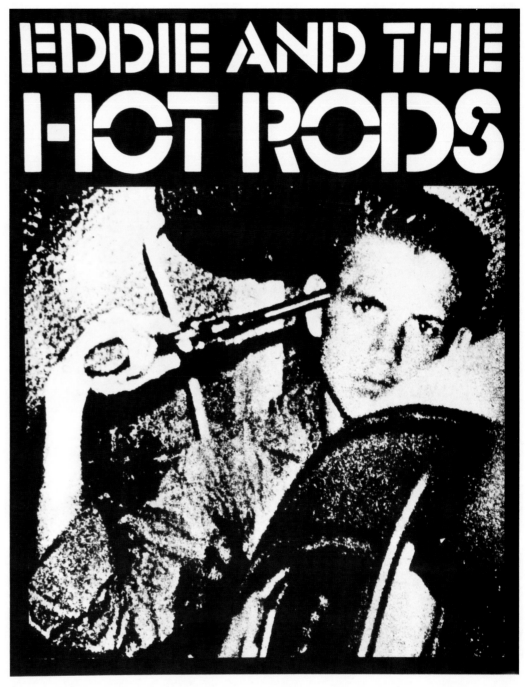

Rock band Be-Bop Deluxe played the pub-rock circuit as punk emerged, and the nihilistic imagery and simple, pared-down rendering of this 1974 poster (above left) promoting their *Axe Victim* album already hinted at a move towards a punk aesthetic.

The poster for Eddie and the Hot Rods – one of the pub-rock bands that laid the foundations for UK punk – was designed by Michael Beal for Island Records. Based on a photograph from the American *True Detective* magazine, which showed a youth threatening to shoot himself, the poster (above right) was created for the band's gig posters, their 1976 single 'Wooly Bully' and, most aptly, their 1977 debut album *Teenage Depression*.

Above left
The Garden, Penzance,
September 1974

Above right
Eddie and the Hot Rods
[Michael Beal],
1976

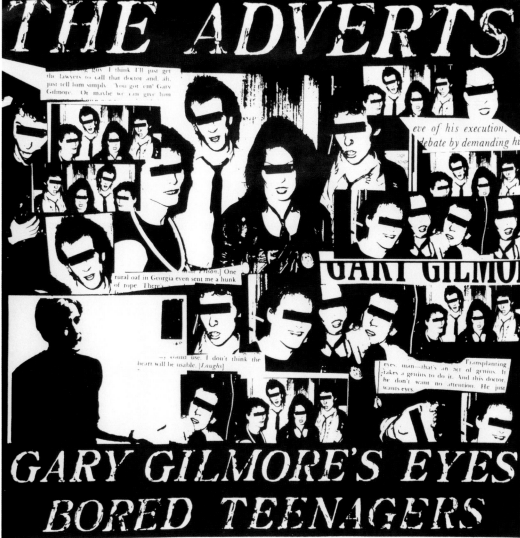

As the fledgling punk scene came of age, new venues like the Roxy and the Vortex in London provided bands with small, intimate stages to vent from. Like the cash-strapped independent record labels, these venues designed their own artwork, using cut-up images and photocopiers to create a home-made style instantly recognizable as punk. Posters and flyers were usually black and white, as shown above in these singles promotions for the UK Subs, on City Records, and the Adverts, on Anchor.

However, this monochrome convention was bucked by designer Barry Jones, who used an early colour photocopier for his Roxy Club flyers, shown opposite. The Roxy, which opened its doors in January 1977 and closed them again in April 1978, managed to produce two live albums featuring songs from early punk acts, such as the UK Subs and the Adverts.

Above left
'I Live in a Car' promotional poster,
September 1978

Above right
'Gary Gilmore's Eyes' promotional poster,
August 1977

Despite having the financial backing of a major record label, the Clash's artwork reflected the stark message of urban decay and dissatisfaction featured in the band's music. The Clash were often pictured in unglamorous and anonymous settings, as shown in the above photo by Kate Simon, shot outside the band's rehearsal studio door in Camden. Posters with a blank strip were distributed by the band's label so information about the record's release could be written by hand in the store.

For the Clash's first single, 'White Riot', Caroline Coon photographed the band 'up against the wall', in a (not so) covert indictment of the police 'stop and search' laws, employed so heavy-handedly during the seventies and partly responsible for the 1976 Notting Hill riots – the subject of 'White Riot'.

Above left
The Clash album and concert poster [Photography: Kate Simon], April 1977

Above right
'White Riot' promotional poster [Photography: Caroline Coon], March 1977

The Clash's third album, *London Calling*, featured a Pennie Smith photo of Paul Simonon smashing his bass guitar on stage. Designed by Ray Lowry, this cover was a homage to Elvis Presley's debut album, created with a black and white photograph and an identical typeface in pink and green (although this alternative green version was used for the promotional poster).

Cut the Crap was the group's final album, and is regarded by many Clash purists as a Joe Strummer solo record, having been recorded after both Topper Headon and Mick Jones had left the band. Designed to exploit the band's hard-won punk credentials, the artwork is a mash-up of punk clichés.

Above left
London Calling promotional poster [Ray Lowry; photography: Pennie Smith], December 1979

Above right
Cut the Crap promotional poster, November 1985

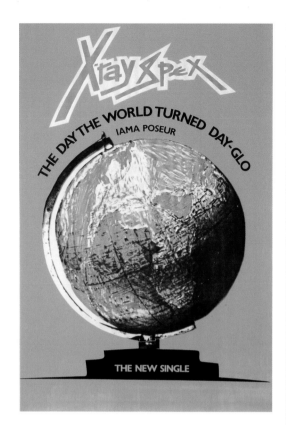

X-Ray Spex singer Poly Styrene designed both of the band's single sleeves from which these posters were adapted. For 'The Day the World Turned Day-Glo' she coloured in a black and white globe with fluorescent felt-tip pens. Poly Styrene explained: 'The Day-Glo poster/record sleeve was done by using a black and white photograph of a globe taken by Falcon Stuart. I then cut it out and coloured it in with day-glo felt-tip pens, ran it though a colour xerox machine, then pasted it onto green day-glo card. The graphic writing was done by hand, by Sophia Horgan.' The poster for X-Ray Spex's debut single 'Oh Bondage! Up Yours!' featured a photograph taken at the Roxy Club, and was done 'in pretty much the same way, but without the felt-tip pens'.

Above left
'The Day the World Turned Day-Glo' promotional poster [Poly Styrene], March 1978

Above right
'Oh Bondage! Up Yours!' promotional poster [Poly Styrene], October 1977

ALTERNATIVE TV

HOW MUCH LONGER YOU BASTARD

Above left
'How Much Longer'
promotional poster,
November 1977

Above right
Power in the Darkness
promotional poster
[Photography: Terry O'Neill],
May 1978

Not everyone was happy simply to shout incoherently; radical political views were equally prevalent. Alternative TV were formed by Mark Perry, founding editor of the seminal fanzine *Sniffin' Glue*, which documented the original punk manifesto and established many of the typographical conventions of punk, from its first issue in July 1976.

The poster for the Tom Robinson Band (with a photograph by Terry O'Neill) promoting their debut album *Power in the Darkness*, heralds the band's active political stance through their logo of a clenched fist – a symbol used throughout history by political groups and oppressed peoples to show defiance and solidarity.

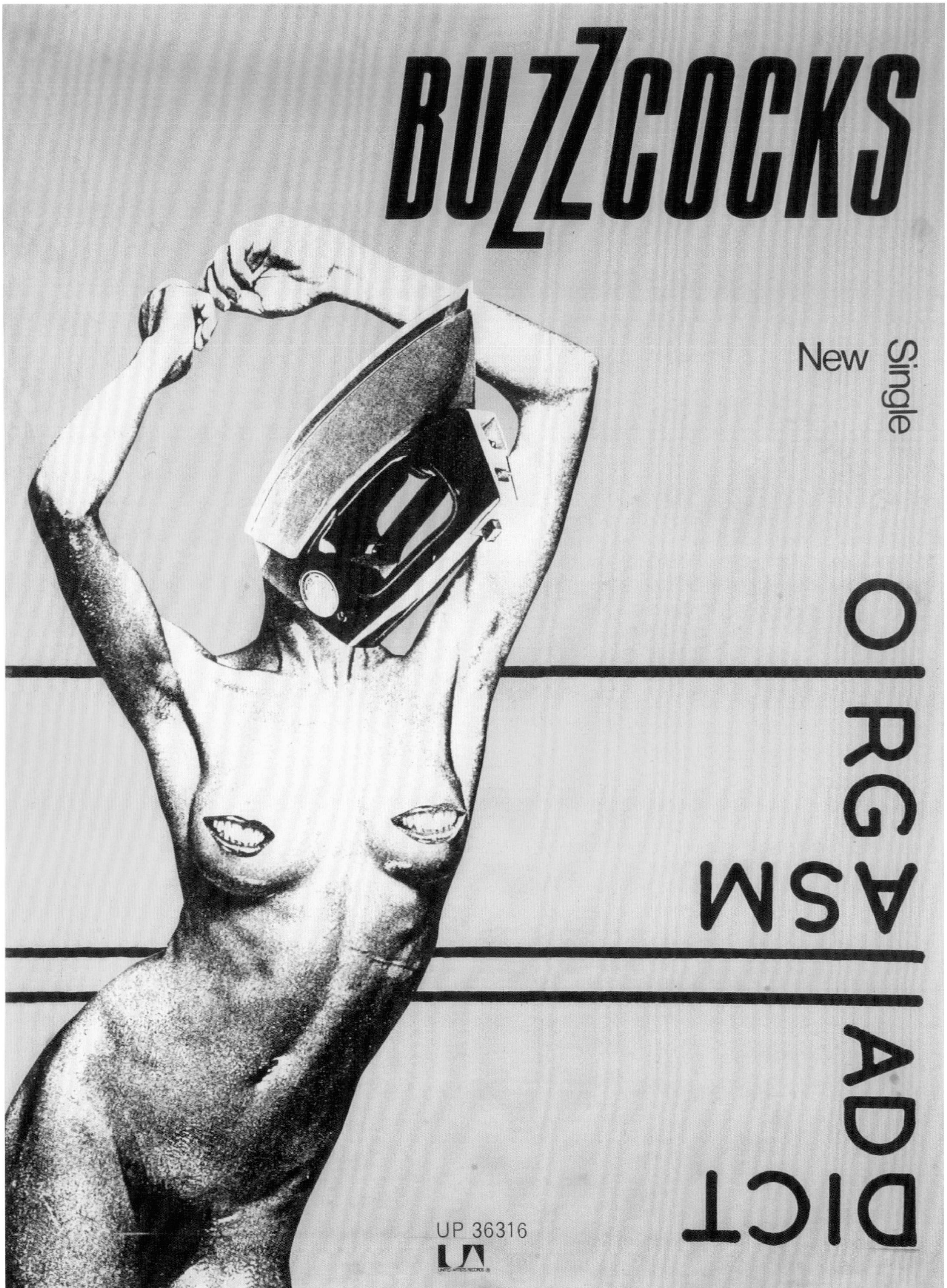

BUZZCOCKS

New Single

ORGASM ADDICT

UP 36316

UNITED ARTISTS RECORDS

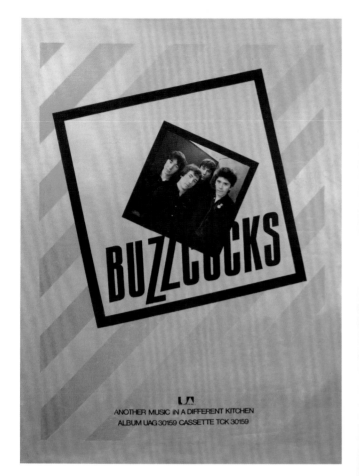

Opposite
'Orgasm Addict' promotional
poster [Malcolm Garrett/
Linder Sterling],
October 1977

Above left
*Another Music in a Different
Kitchen* promotional poster
[Malcolm Garrett],
March 1978

Above right
'What Do I Get?' promotional
poster [Malcolm Garrett],
February 1978

After studying graphics at Manchester
Polytechnic (alongside Peter Saville),
Malcolm Garrett became involved in
the local punk scene as the regular
designer for the Buzzcocks' promotional
material. The image on the group's
debut single, 'Orgasm Addict', was
based on a montage by feminist artist
Linder Sterling, a well-known figure
from the Manchester punk scene.
Sterling's artworks often combined
pornographic images of women with
pictures of household appliances
taken from women's magazines.

With his work for the Sex Pistols, featuring cut-up 'ransom note' lettering, artist Jamie Reid refined the graphic style of UK punk rock. While attending Croydon Art School he had met the Pistols' future manager Malcolm McLaren, and went on to create the group's early promotional material. These included the ripped Union Jack poster for the sleeve of 'Anarchy in the UK', and the sleeve and posters for 'God Save the Queen' (based on a famous photograph by Cecil Beaton), which Sean O'Hagan described in *The Observer* as 'the single most iconic image of the punk era'.

Opposite top
'Anarchy in the UK' promotional poster [Jamie Reid], November 1976

Opposite below
Never Mind the Bollocks flyer [in the style of Jamie Reid], October 1977

Top
'God Save the Queen' promotional poster [Jamie Reid], May 1977

Above left
'Holidays in the Sun' promotional poster [Jamie Reid], October 1977

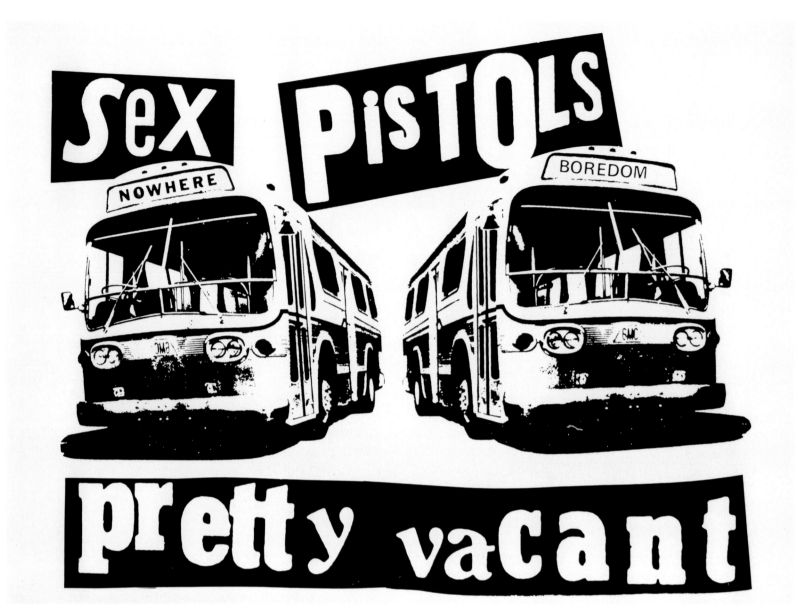

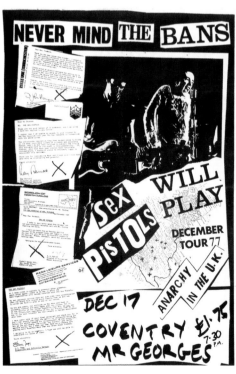

Top
'Pretty Vacant' promotional
poster [Jamie Reid],
July 1977

Left
'Never Mind the Bans'
flyer [Jamie Reid],
December 1977

Jamie Reid's 'Pretty Vacant' image appeared on the back of the sleeve for the Sex Pistols' single, having already been used by Reid (with 'Nowhere' as the destination of both buses) for the Situationist magazine *Suburban Press* in 1972. The single was released during the height of the band's notoriety, at which time they were banned from performing in the UK. Such was the popularity of the band that their manager Malcolm McLaren sought to exploit their earning potential, even to the point of ridiculing the band's anarchistic image – much to the disgust of singer Johnny Rotten, who subsequently left the band.

Top
The Great Rock 'n' Roll Swindle
promotional poster,
February 1979

Below
The Great Rock 'n' Roll Swindle
promotional poster,
February 1979

Button badges first appeared as part of rock fashion during the late 1960s hippy era, displaying (often humorous) statements such as 'Legalize Pot', 'Support Your Local Poet' and 'Save Water – Bath With A Friend', as well as the occasional band or album promotion. But they really came into their own in the seventies, when record companies and bands produced large numbers of button badges displaying their logos, names and album graphics. As part of the safety-pin punk look, fans would proudly plaster their jackets, hats and bags with the badges to show off their punk credentials and affiliations.

Originally marketed as a punk band
wearing sharp suits, the Jam are seen
above in a poster for their debut album
In The City (with the photo-within-a-
photo taken by Martyn Goddard).
As their musical inspirations became
more influenced by the mod movement
of the 1960s, so did their marketing
material. The design for the poster
(above right) for the Jam's 1980 album,
Sound Affects, harks back to the
sixties pop art era.

    Similarly, the Only Ones ditched
their punk imagery for the 'Planet Tour'
poster shown opposite, which features
a 1950s horror-movie style typeface
that was not used elsewhere by them;
the dinosaur borrowed from the same
movie genre was also a quirky one-off.

Above left
In The City promotional poster
[Bill Smith; photography: Martyn
Goddard],
May 1977

Above right
Sound Affects promotional
poster,
November 1980

Opposite
'Planet Tour' poster [Kavanagh],
April 1978

The ONLY ONES

PLANET TOUR

Calling itself 'The World's Most Flexible Record Label', Stiff emerged as one of the most successful new labels formed in the wake of the punk revolution. Signing an eclectic mix of bands and solo artists, Stiff created amusing and provocative slogans to market itself and its acts, including: 'If it Ain't Stiff, it Ain't Worth a F**k' and 'We came. We saw. We left.'

On the 1978 'Be Stiff' tour the entire package travelled from venue to venue in a specially hired railway train, hence the 'Travel By Train' poster. The label's roster included punk band the Damned, the psychedelic Pink Fairies, pub-rockers Roogalator, solo rock 'n' roller Nick Lowe, and quirky vocalists Lene Lovich and Wreckless Eric. The poster shown above right was created by Stiff's original art director, Chris Morton, in celebration of the first eight singles to be released by the label.

Above left
'Be Stiff' tour poster
[Photography: Chris Gabrin],
October 1978

Above right
Stiff Records promotional poster
[Chris Morton],
November 1976

Below right
'Live Stiffs' tour poster
[Chris Morton; photography:
Chris Gabrin],
October 1977

Elvis Costello

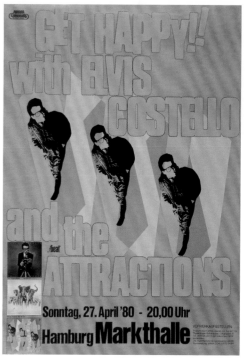

Above left
Stiff Records promotional
poster [Barney Bubbles;
photography: Chris Gabrin],
October 1977

Above right
My Aim Is True promotional
poster [Barney Bubbles;
photography: Keith Morris],
July 1977

Below right
Markthalle, Hamburg
[Barney Bubbles;
photography: Chris Gabrin],
April 1980

Elvis Costello was Stiff's most
successful signing and the label was
instrumental in helping create the
bespectacled singer's 'punk Buddy
Holly' image through highly original
album covers and promotional material.
The debut album *My Aim Is True*, above
right, promoted Costello as 'Buddy
Holly on acid'. The green-and-yellow
poster, above left, was one of a series
created to promote Stiff's star acts;
others featured Ian Dury and Nick Lowe.

BARNEY BUBBLES

Although his most famous images, both on record covers and poster art, have been associated with the new wave of music that followed in the wake of punk at the end of the seventies, Barney Bubbles' work transcended genres, going back to the psychedelic era of a decade earlier.

Born Colin Fulcher in 1942, in Isleworth, London, Bubbles embarked on his studies in display and packaging at Twickenham College of Art in 1958; the cardboard design aspects of the latter undoubtedly influencing his future activities in record covers. After a stint with the Conran Group as senior package designer in the mid-1960s, Bubbles got involved with the London hippy counterculture during the 'Summer of Love' year of 1967, where he operated under the name of Barney Bubbles – a name he later adopted officially. Bubbles ran a light show for various bands, including Gun and Quintessence, in the new 'underground' venues such as the Roundhouse, the Arts Lab and Middle Earth.

More significantly, Bubbles was also a part-time contributor to the seminal *Oz* magazine as well as other underground publications, and in 1968 he spent some time in the epicentre of hippy culture, San Francisco. Here, he got to know some of the leading psychedelic poster designers, including Stanley Mouse and Alton Kelley, and worked on light shows at the city's famous Avalon Ballroom.

After returning to London in 1969, Bubbles became a partner in Teenburger Designs, for which he co-designed his first record sleeve, the album *In Blissful Company* by Quintessence. (With its gatefold sleeve and booklet, this album was a forerunner of many of the ambitious packages that would form part of the Barney Bubbles trademark style.) Other bands began to use Teenburger for album design, including the leading pub-rock act Brinsley Schwarz.

At the time, Bubbles was also working on the design of the underground paper *Friends*, through which he met the 'space rock' band Hawkwind. Bubbles and Hawkwind enjoyed a highly fruitful collaboration through the first half of the seventies, producing LP sleeves, posters, press advertisements and stage designs. It was Bubbles' richest body of work of the pre-punk period, during which he also produced sleeves and posters for a number of bands, including Edgar Broughton, Quiver and the Kursaal Flyers. In 1972 he created the triple album package *Glastonbury Fayre*, with a six-panel fold-out sleeve, two posters and a booklet, all presented in a clear plastic holder.

When UK punk exploded in 1976, several new independent record labels appeared, including Stiff Records, set up by Dave Robinson and Jake Riviera. Early in 1977 they employed Barney to help create a fresh and dynamic image for the label, with sleeves for artists including the Damned, Elvis Costello and Ian Dury and the Blockheads, as well as promotional material for the label itself. Apart from the Damned and the Adverts, most of the Stiff artists weren't out-and-out punk acts, but part of the new wave that regenerated UK pop in the late seventies. Key Barney Bubbles artworks from the period included Costello, legs apart, wielding his guitar on *My Aim Is True*, and the deconstructed 'spotted dog' toy on Ian Dury's 'Hit Me With Your Rhythm Stick' single – plus, of course, the famous 'face' logo created for Dury's Blockheads.

'Bubbles broke out of the commercial constraints of his given trade and emerged as a pure artist, one whose silent influence lingers.'
Paul Gorman, *Reasons To Be Cheerful* (Adelita Books, 2008)

The first single
(I want to be an) anglepoise lamp
Fat Man's Son
ADA 8
The first tour
May
25 London Marquee
26 London Nashville
27 High Wycombe Nags Head
31 Sheffield Limit Club
June
2 Middlesborough Rock Garden
5 Edinburgh Tiffany's
7 Newport Stowaways Club
8 Leeds Roots
9 Manchester Rafters
15 Plymouth Metro
17 Portsmouth Polytechnic
18 London Marquee

Radarscope Ltd trading as Radar Records
In association with WEA Records Ltd
A Warner Communications Company

ake Riviera departed Stiff to set up Radar Records in 1978 (followed by F-Beat Records in 980), taking Stiff stars Costello and Nick Lowe with him – and Barney Bubbles. While continuing to design for some Stiff artists, Bubbles' work for Radar and F-Beat – including Costello, Lowe, Carlene Carter and others – was among his best known. Barney also designed for other labels throughout the ate seventies and early eighties, creating memorable magery on sleeves, posters and flyers for a host of contemporary artists, including Johnny Moped, Dr Feelgood, Billy Bragg and the Psychedelic Furs.

In the words of his biographer Paul Gorman: Barney Bubbles' greatest achievement may have been his fast-tracking of vanguard ideas into the mainstream. In grey mid-1970s Britain he communicated lesser-known aspects of "culture" – rt Deco, Constructivism, concrete poetry

Expressionism, post-Modernism, whatever – via the mass media of record sleeves, posters, adverts, ephemera and art direction for the mass-market publication NME.'

Following bouts of depression initiated by financial and personal problems, not to mention the deaths of both of his parents, Barney committed suicide in 1983. His art was unique, rich in symbolism, and made full use of ciphers such as stars, crowns and circles; he played with geometry and form, and his work was littered with references to art and musical history, influencing innumerable artists working in rock-related graphics since.

As Gorman summed up: 'He was a truly alternative artist, a radical thinker who did not, or could not, conform to even the staple artistic stance of signature and recognition, yet was at his most effective working within commercial strictures'.

Above
Soft Boys single and tour poster
[Barney Bubbles],
May 1978

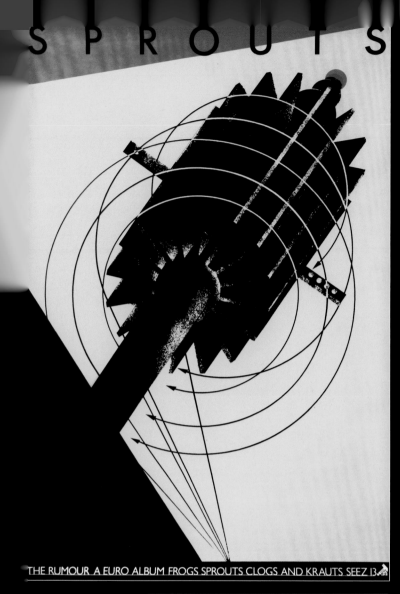

THE RUMOUR A EURO ALBUM FROGS SPROUTS CLOGS AND KRAUTS SEEZ 13

Above left
Frogs, Clogs, Sprouts and Krauts promotional poster [Barney Bubbles], March 1969

Below left
Blockheads logo

Above right
The Ian Dury Songbook book cover [Barney Bubbles], 1979

Below right
Music For Pleasure (The Damned) sleeve design

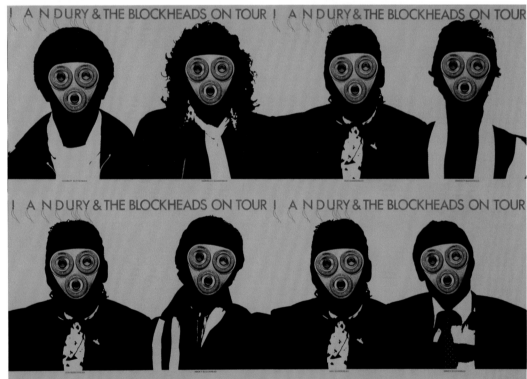

Above left
New Boots and Panties!!
promotional poster
[Barney Bubbles;
photography: Chris Gabrin],
September 1977

Above right
Do It Yourself promotional
poster [Barney Bubbles],
May 1979

Below
Ian Dury & the Blockheads tour
poster [Barney Bubbles],
1979

Ian Dury & the Blockheads were another act associated with the work of Barney Bubbles. Dury, who worked closely with Bubbles on the band's art, remembered him as 'easily the most incredible designer I'd ever come across.' Bubbles designed the cover art for the band's 1979 *Do It Yourself* (the promotional poster for the album is shown above), which was released with 28 different sleeves, each one based on a different Crown Wallpaper design. Dury is pictured in a photo by Chris Gabrin on the poster for the band's debut album, *New Boots and Panties!!*, which were the only two items of clothing he insisted on buying new.

Right
New Boots and Panties!!
promotional poster
[Barney Bubbles;
photography: Chris Gabrin],
September 1977

The title of Squeeze's *Cool for Cats* single and album was taken from a 1950s UK TV pop music show. The styling of the album cover and promotional poster was in a similarly retro vein, harking back to the 'beat' graphics of that time in its design.

The Psychedelic Furs poster, promoting their single 'We Love You', was created by the group's singer, ex-art student Richard Butler, who today exhibits his art in galleries around the world. Formed in 1977, the Psychedelic Furs were one of the longer-lasting bands from the punk era, surviving until 1991 before splitting up and then reforming in 2000.

Above left
Cool for Cats promotional poster,
March 1979

Above right
'We Love You' promotional poster [Richard Butler],
October 1979

Following closely on the heels of punk and new wave was a ska and bluebeat revival, led by Coventry bands the Specials, the Selecter and others on the 2-Tone label – named after the fabric used in 1960s mod fashion. 2-Tone also took artwork inspiration from the mod era, and its monotone style (in evidence in the posters shown opposite) was reminiscent of the Biba prints. Chiswick Records, which had pioneered the indie scene immediately before the advent of punk, was the home of R&B band Red Beans & Rice, another UK 'mod revival' outfit from the early 1980s.

BRIT ROCK TO BRIT POP

INTO THE MAINSTREAM

The 1970s saw a rise in lengthy record-company-sponsored tours by the biggest names in British rock music, including the Rolling Stones and the Who. These tours would incorporate multiple dates and be promoted by new and innovative poster art. The studios and artists producing this artwork – at the time largely unnamed and unacknowledged – are today credited as major contributors to British rock illustration.

During the same era, heavy metal became a global phenomenon, bringing with it the instantly recognizable imagery of bands such as Black Sabbath, Iron Maiden and Motörhead, and their custom-designed logos, typefaces and illustrations. This heavy metal branding had album design at its core, but it also spawned a plethora of spin-off graphic material, from album pull-outs to flyers, as well as tour promotional material and decorative posters.

In the 1980s, music was becoming a more corporate affair and, with the advent of CDs and the launch of MTV, artists were coaxed off tour and back into the recording studio. As a result, the artwork produced for mainstream rock bands such as Simple Minds, Culture Club and Duran Duran centred largely on album covers rather than concert posters.

Towards the end of the century, rock festivals, hitherto rooted in the counterculture of the late sixties, became something of a cultural institution. As the festivals turned into large, sponsored events, so the promotional material became less 'artistic', with the more imaginative poster artwork often relegated to the smaller, independently organized events.

By the 1990s, big business had taken control, as most of the 'indie' record labels either went bust or were assimilated into the bigger companies. These multinationals sought to consolidate their investment by styling rock acts as brands, with strong identities that were designed to create recognition and foster loyalty amongst the fans. While some of the larger independent labels, such as Factory and Island records, continued to produce ground-breaking art, many of the majors also set up small satellite labels with their own catalogue of bands – these bore a superficial resemblance to the indies, but they were actually part of huge corporations. During the nineties, Brit pop took centre stage. Bands such as Oasis and Pulp created logo-led designs for their album and poster art, while contemporaries Blur opted for more of a mix of styles, with illustrations by graffiti artist Banksy.

Formerly the Finsbury Park Astoria cinema, London's Rainbow Theatre was one of the leading venues for rock during the 1970s. The Astoria fell under the auspices of John Morris, whose pedigree in event production included the Woodstock Festival and the Fillmore East in New York. The venue used a signature trademark logo on all of its posters, as shown above, although the posters themselves were created by a variety of different designers; the designers of these two posters are unidentified.

Above left
Artwork for Rainbow Theatre, Finsbury Park, London, February 1972

Above right
Rainbow Theatre, Finsbury Park, London, March 1972

A number of the Rolling Stones' tour posters were designed by John Pasche (who created their trademark 'lips' logo in 1971), including several that were inspired by pre-war travel posters. Pasche comments: 'The decision to go with a pastiche of a travel poster for the Stones' 1970 tour came out of an initial meeting/brief with Mick Jagger. We wanted to create an image which was different from the usual band shot, and focus more on the idea of touring. The style came out of a mutual interest of the thirties and forties travel posters. A bit of a twist was putting the Concorde in there. I airbrushed the image using concentrated colour inks on high white art board.'

The unusual round poster (right) promoted the Rolling Stones' 1976 gig at one of the UK's biggest festivals, the Knebworth Fair.

Above left
Rolling Stones American Tour poster [John Pasche], June–July 1972

Above right
Rolling Stones European Tour poster [John Pasche], August–October 1970

Right
Knebworth Fair [Walker-Parkinson Design], August 1976

Above
Earl's Court, London
[Martine Grainey],
May 1975

Led Zeppelin manager Peter Grant and promoter Mel Bush came up with the 'Zeppelin Express' to advertise the band's 1975 appearances at Earl's Court Arena in London. This promotional poster features the Zeppelin train and a timetable to get fans from all over the country to the gig. The poster, together with the programme for the concerts, was designed by Martine Grainey of Peter Grainey Graphics in Bournemouth. Influenced by the flowing style of Art Nouveau, Grainey's poster designs were also reproduced on glass, with a small number silvered in the style of bar mirrors to present to band members after the event. The Zeppelin poster is Grainey's favourite: 'Led Zeppelin were the kings of rock in the seventies and it was so evident that other bands were drawing their inspiration from them.'

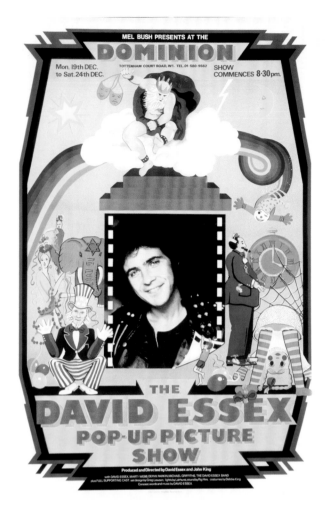

As well as designing for Led Zeppelin, Martine Grainey created a number of other high-profile concert posters during 1975, including teen idol David Essex's 'All the Fun of the Fair' Autumn UK tour and his 'Pop-Up Picture Show' at the Dominion Theatre, London. Grainey also designed the poster for a package show at Wembley Stadium, headlined by Elton John, the Beach Boys and the Eagles.

Above left
David Essex, Pop-Up Picture Show, Dominion Theatre, London [Martine Grainey], December 1975

Above right
David Essex, All the Fun of the Fair UK Tour [Martine Grainey], September–October 1975

Below right
Elton John, Midsummer Music Show, Wembley Stadium [Martine Grainey], June 1975

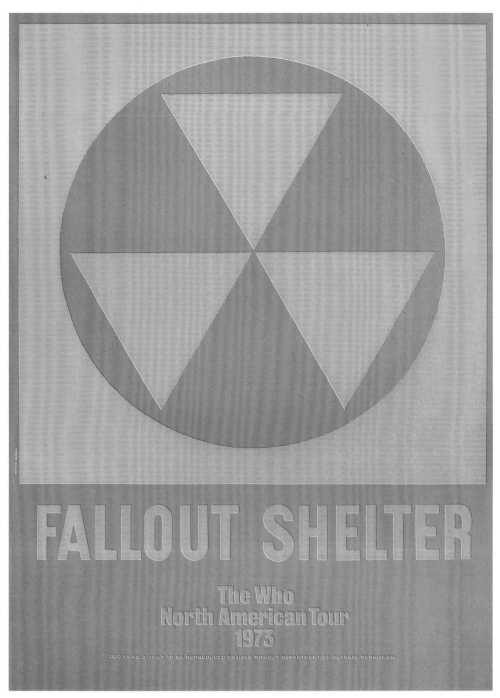

FALLOUT SHELTER

The Who
North American Tour
1973

DOD FS NO. 2 (NOT TO BE REPRODUCED OR USED WITHOUT DEPARTMENT OF DEFENSE PERMISSION)

THE WHO 1981

WHO TOUR 1981

673
Paint the Town
Green

14 ml

With its bold blocks of text and colour and sans serif type, the Who poster (above) typifies the graphic style of designer and Soviet poster collector David King. Lending his talents to political activism, King also designed the arrow logo for the British Anti-Nazi League. As a shoe designer in the early 1970s, Richard Evans put multi-coloured platforms under the feet of rock dignitaries like Elton John, George Harrison and Roxy Music, before working with Aubrey Powell and Storm Thorgerson as a graphic designer at Hipgnosis. Evans has worked for the Who since 1976, styling everything from album covers to tour merchandise.

Above left
The Who 1973 North American Tour poster [David King], November 1973

Above right
The Who 1981 tour programme [Richard Evans], January 1981

Below right
The Who 1981 tour merchandise [Richard Evans], January 1981

HUGH GILMOUR

One of most respected artists in the field today, Hugh Gilmour has designed album covers, merchandise and posters for Iron Maiden, Deep Purple, Motörhead, Alice Cooper, Bruce Dickinson and Whitesnake, among other leading metal names. He has also created artworks for the Who, the Beatles, David Bowie and the Sex Pistols. However, his greatest passion has always been for heavy metal, and it was this that brought him into the music industry in the first place.

Gilmour recalls: 'I was at Kingston College of Art for a year, then got a summer job at a record label called Castle Communications, which didn't have a very good reputation – it was best known for things like budget CDs. But they also had some stuff that I really liked, back catalogue material of Led Zepp, Black Sabbath, and beyond that, the Pye catalogue, for instance, so they had the Kinks, and so on. So, I could see that they had this amazing catalogue, and certainly their packaging didn't do the product justice. So I got to work on Black Sabbath reissues.'

Being a dedicated metal fan as well as a graphic designer, Gilmour has definite views about aspects of heavy metal imagery, and how it came about: 'Using Black Sabbath as an example, a lot of the sleeves, if you look at them now, it might be iconic or classic, but really, if you analyze it, you think, "what were they thinking?" I mean, the *Paranoid* sleeve, for instance, it might be iconic, but this guy in a pink jump suit and blue underpants, waving a sword with a crash helmet on – I understand that was designed when it was going to be called 'Warpigs', and,

apparently, this guy's a Warpig – but it's still a strange image. Or the *Sabotage* album, where the band's on the cover – Ozzy Osbourne's wearing a kimono, and Phil Ward, you can see his chequered red underpants through his wife's red tights – so what was going through their minds, I don't know. At the same time I love their sleeves like *Technical Ecstasy* (1976), and *Sabbath Bloody Sabbath* is very much a heavy metal illustration. When I was at Kingston, a guy called Geoff Halpin gave a lecture, and it turns out that he did a lot of logos for Hipgnosis, a lot of the typography. And one of the bands he worked with was Black Sabbath, he actually did the Teutonic, almost Nazi-looking lettering for Sabbath, and he actually felt responsible for giving heavy metal this Teutonic image that it didn't have before. Before that, Led Zeppelin didn't have these weird images. But bands like Motörhead certainly adopted it in a big style.'

Gilmour elaborates: 'But I think the band that got their sleeves so right was Iron Maiden, with the logo, which has remained relatively unchanged, with slight variance, for 32 years. And, of course, Eddie always plays a part somehow. I think the fans would be very disappointed – I'd be very disappointed – if Eddie didn't appear in some fashion. But the whole sword and sorcery thing, if you look at the work of Frank Frazetta . . . it predates his work being used for album sleeves; he did a lot of Conan the Barbarian and classic illustration from the fifties and sixties onwards. But it's all very macho, with women with heaving bosoms, and essentially it appeals to a 14-year-old boy's pubescent yearnings – that's the appeal of a lot of the artwork in heavy metal.'

'If truth be told, I joined Castle Communications PLC solely because they had Black Sabbath's catalogue AND it looked awful, but specifically because it looked awful. One day it would have to be re-done more sensitively, restoring the integrity of the original packaging and artwork, and maybe adding extra elements if possible, and I was going to make sure I was there when it happened.'

Hugh Gilmour, *Confessions of a Black Sabbath Fan* (www.iommi.com)

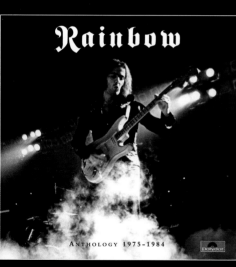

Top left
Tony Iommi *Fused* album cover
[Hugh Gilmour],
July 2005

Centre left
Diamond Head *The MCA Years*
box set cover [Hugh Gilmour],
August 2009

Below left
Rainbow *Anthology*
1975–1984 album cover
[Hugh Gilmour],
September 2009

Above right
Led Zeppelin *Mothership*
promotional poster [Hugh
Gilmour/Shepard Fairey],
November 2007

BRONSKI BEAT · TRUTHDARE DOUBLEDARE

FEATURING **HIT THAT PERFECT BEAT** + **C'MON! C'MON!** + **IN MY DREAMS**

MCA RECORDS

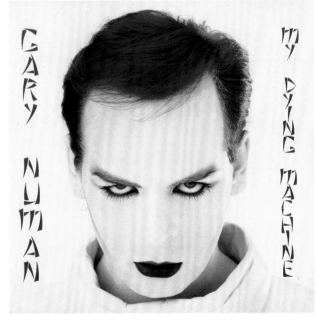

The eighties saw a resurgence of interest in German electronica pioneers, Kraftwerk, whose minimal distillation of dance beats was a welcome alternative to some of the overworked productions of the big eighties bands. The LCD-style type on the 'Pocket Calculator' poster (above right) echoed the growing popularity of all things digital at that time. Bronski Beat added their own high-energy take on electronica, with singer Jimmy Somerville doing a fine impression of 1970s disco superstar Sylvester.

Above left
Bronski Beat *Truthdare Doubledare* promotional poster [Pete Barrett/Andrew Biscomb], 1986

Above right
Kraftwerk 'Pocket Calculator' single promotional poster, May 1981

Below right
Gary Numan 'My Dying Machine' single cover [Francis Drake/Fraser Gray], October 1984

tears for fears *the seeds of love*
the album compact disc, cassette and l.p.
includes sowing the seeds of love
★★★★★ **Q** REVIEW October 1989

With CD sales being hugely profitable, record companies were keen to fund bands to perfect their sound in the recording studio, rather than through live performances. With all the focus being on the recorded product, posters were often reproductions of album or single art, rather than creations in their own right. In many cases, record covers or videos became the closest contact fans had with bands.

Above left
Tears For Fears *The Seeds of Love* promotional poster [Stylorouge],
September 1989

Above right
Siouxsie and the Banshees *Once Upon A Time* promotional poster [Stylorouge],
December 1981

Below right
ABC 'How to Be a Millionaire' single promotional poster [Keith Breeden],
January 1985

MALCOLM GARRETT

With his design company Assorted Images, Malcolm Garrett was hugely influential in the development of rock graphics during the early 1980s era of post-punk pop.

Born in Northwich in 1956, Garrett studied typography at Reading University from 1974–75. Following this, he returned to his native North West and enrolled on the Graphic Design course at Manchester Polytechnic – there, he was reunited with his old school friend, Peter Saville, who would go on to make his own mark on rock design with Factory Records. Although he was only at Reading for a short time, Malcolm acquired what he describes as an 'academic grounding' in the history of typography, and 20th-century typographic design in particular: 'I did come back with books about [typography pioneer] Jan Tschichold. And I'd spent a lot of time in the library at Reading University looking at typography books, so I had given myself a grounding. I felt I knew everything about typography at that point . . . in my naive youth kind of way.'

It was while he was at Manchester Poly that Garrett met Linder Sterling, who was studying illustration in the year above him, and through her formed what would become a highly successful relationship with local punk band the Buzzcocks. 'She went to see the Buzzcocks, they were just a pub band, and got to know Howard Devoto. He was still the singer in the band then, and they asked me to design a poster to advertise gigs. So I just got to know them.'

It was the collaboration between Sterling and Garrett that produced one of the most iconic images in British rock, the famous montage of a woman with an iron for a head that appeared on the sleeve of the Buzzcocks' single 'Orgasm Addict': 'Linder had done a variety of montages, and we decided we'd use that particular one on the record sleeve, so I took it away and designed the record sleeve around it.' In the process, Garrett also created a logo for the band. 'From the early seventies, bands did have logos, but they were all complex, horrible affairs . . . I was more interested in the overall visual identity, of which having a lettering style was a part.'

As his work for the Buzzcocks became more extensive, a variety of company names evolved that eventually became Assorted Images. 'I used the name Arbitrary Images as the credit on the first record sleeve that I did for Buzzcocks, and I kept changing the name, just through the desire to have fun. Then Richard Boon, the Buzzcocks' manager, had occasion to . . . send me some information for a new sleeve, and he addressed it to "Assorted Images" because he picked up on the idea that I'd been using an assortment of names.'

After moving to London and freelancing for a couple of years, Garrett went into partnership with Kasper De Graaf and established their company as Assorted Images. Garrett explains: 'He'd been Features Editor at *Smash Hits*, and he'd done a magazine about Duran Duran and Spandau Ballet and the whole New Romantic thing, called *New Sounds New Styles*. He'd done it as a one-off; it was successful, and the publisher liked it and said we should launch it as a monthly magazine. So he approached me, as somebody who understood the target audience, to design the magazine.'

'What pop art had managed to do was simplify commercial art, make it more beautiful, get to its essential purity – so then we took it back into commercial art.'
Malcolm Garrett, 2010

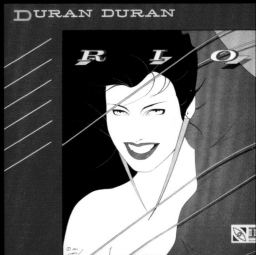

Top
Duran Duran 'The Reflex' single
cover [Assorted Images],
April 1984

Below left
Culture Club *Colour By
Numbers* album cover
[Assorted Images],
October 1983

Below right
Duran Duran *Rio* album cover
[Assorted Images],
May 1982

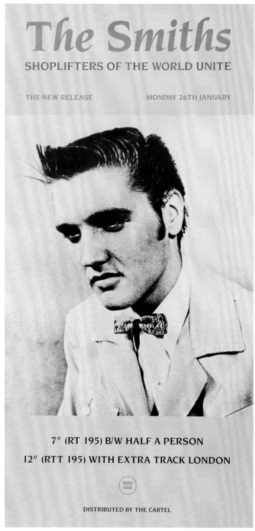

Conceived by lead singer Morrissey, the Smiths' records and posters employed enigmatic vintage black and white, tinted photographs to give a sense of authenticity and integrity, while the oblique relevance lent the band an air of mystery. The posters above show (from left) a 1961 photo of English playwright Shelagh Delaney, a 1954 photo of Elvis Presley and a picture of teenagers from *Rock 'n' Roll Times* by the Hamburg photographer, Jürgen Vollmer.

For their instantly recognizable look, Oasis' posters were straight copies of their record covers (designed by Brian Cannon at Microdot) plus their familiar logo, mimicking the style of the 'red-top' tabloid newspapers they so often found themselves the subject of.

Above left
The Smiths 'Girlfriend in a Coma' single promotional poster [Morrissey],
August 1987

Above centre
The Smiths 'Shoplifters of the World Unite' single promotional poster [Morrissey],
January 1987

Above right
The Smiths *The World Won't Listen* promotional poster [Morrissey],
February 1987

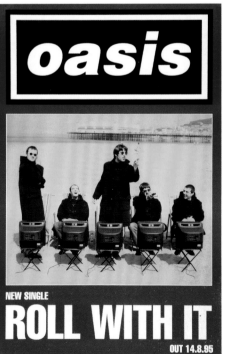

Above left
Oasis *Definitely Maybe*
promotional poster [Microdot],
August 1994

Above right
Oasis 'Cigarettes & Alcohol'
single promotional poster
[Microdot],
October 1994

Below left
Oasis 'Don't Look Back In
Anger' single promotional poster
[Microdot],
February 1996

Below right
Oasis 'Roll With It' single
promotional poster [Microdot],
August 1995

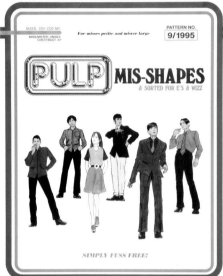

Other major names in the nineties Brit pop stakes included Pulp and Blur. Pulp's distinctive logo, which featured on all their packaging and promotional material, was created by Designers Republic, while Blur's 1994 *Parklife* album and the above promotional poster for a 2009 Hyde Park gig, were both designed by Stylorouge.

Above left
Pulp 'Common People'
single cover,
June 1995

Below left
Pulp 'Mis-Shapes' single
promotional poster,
September 1995

Above right
Blur Hyde Park, London
[Stylorouge],
July 2009

New single 14.04.03
www.blur.co.uk

Above left
Blur *Think Tank* promotional
poster [Banksy],
May 2003

Above right
Blur 'Out Of Time' single
promotional poster [Banksy],
April 2003

Below right
Blur: The Best Of promotional
poster [Julian Opie],
October 2000

Into the 21st century, Blur recruited two
of the biggest names in contemporary
British art for their record artwork. The
secretive graffiti artist Banksy provided
the image for their 2003 album, *Think
Tank*, and the single release from it,
'Out Of Time'. Like Blur guitarist
Graham Coxon, who studied fine art at
Goldsmiths (where his artistic interests
were shared by future band member
Alex James), Julian Opie came from an
art school background and portrayed
the band in his trademark style for the
cover of *Blur: The Best Of* in 2000.

VAUGHAN OLIVER

A naked man twirls his belt of semi-erect eels, cataract-blue cow eyes peer out from a marshmallow landscape, a topless flamenco dancer tilts into a sepia-toned background – the covers are classic Vaughan Oliver; surreal, humorous and dark. Credited as the most innovative post-punk designer of the eighties and nineties, Oliver has created covers for the Pixies, the Cocteau Twins, Frank Black, this Mortal Coil, the Breeders and many more. But to meet Vaughan Oliver can be something of a surprise: 'One guy who met me said he was expecting some sort of dark Tarkovskian prince, but what he got instead was a benign football manager.'

Oliver's 30-year design career – with its accomplishments and credits too long to list on this page – began in his grammar school art room, where conversation focused on football and record covers. 'I liked the idea of someone using their imagination in the way that Roger Dean did. That spoke to me, it treated you with intelligence. I thought, "Wow, this is cool, I want to do this."'

After Newcastle upon Tyne Polytechnic and a stint in design packaging at the studios of Benchmark and Michael Peters & Partners, opportunity knocked for Oliver in a chance encounter with 4AD founder Ivo Watts-Russell. For three years, Watts-Russell would feed work to Oliver, who would insist that 4AD create a strong identity and consistent designs for its bands. So in 1983, Watts-Russell made the young designer his first employee. 'I didn't know how to put a bit of artwork together at the time, I was just learning by trial and error. But Ivo and I shared old-fashioned virtues like care and sense of quality. And in those days it all centred around creative control by the band and the artist. It was a great outlet for young designers.'

Oliver's brief was simple: listen to the demo tapes, read the lyrics and let album-cover inspiration take hold. 'It was all borne of the music and I was getting natural inspiration from it. But I also needed it to be something collectible. I wanted people to be seduced by this package, make it something they wanted to have – to have and to hold.'

Sometimes the bands would give Oliver directives, other times not. At an early Pixies meeting, lead singer Charles Thompson, a.k.a. Frank Black, expressed his fondness for male nudity and David Lynch. The now legendary image for *Come On Pilgrim* presented itself soon afterwards at photographer Simon Larbalestier's Royal College graduation show. 'Here I am looking for male nudity and something "Lynchian", and there was that photo of man with a hairy back just standing there.'

Oliver's legacy is one of collaboration ('It makes it better') and Larbalestier is part of a bench of photographers and designers used for specific projects for Oliver's studios-23 Envelope and later v23. Oliver's closest association is with long-standing right-hand man, Chris Biggs. 'Chris has been with me since '82, he's survived three of my marriages and we've formed a firm relationship. He's central to the whole thing.' Biggs and Oliver are responsible for the thread that runs though all of their 4AD artwork – a feel or style that Oliver says is difficult to define. 'I think it's a use of typography, the texture, an oblique way of looking at things, with a feeling of mystery and ambiguity. A Portuguese student of mine was trying to describe it, and she said, "It's your soul." And I said, "We don't talk like that in this country."'

Oliver's techniques are grounded in the old school of design – layers of imagery and type are often still built up organically on a board rather than on a computer. He is imparting this old-school knowledge to his students at the University of Creative Arts, Epsom, who were enlisted to work on the Pixies *Minotaur* box set. For the project, Oliver scrapped all existing Pixies artwork and asked his students to create logos and designs from things like glue, card and nails, and used them untouched alongside Larbalestier's new photography. Oliver's hands-on methods were also responsible for his pioneering work with typography, which he created in the dark room using a Photo Mechanical Transfer machine to enlarge or reduce type, and manipulate it with different exposure times and chemicals. But the machines are now defunct and Oliver has had – to a point – to embrace Mac technology. 'There's a place for it, but I think finally people have understood there isn't an ideas button on a Mac. Everything starts with an idea, and there are other ways of doing it.'

Oliver is more worried about the technology of downloadable music, which lacks a physical visual representation. It is difficult territory for a designer who has dedicated his life to creating covers for fans 'to have and to hold'. 'I think we need something to objectify the music. We need the collectability of the package – to put the music in a sleeve and put it on a shelf. God knows what's going to happen now with the appearance of eBooks. What are the shelving people going to do?'

'There's a funny thing with all the bands. They say "yeah it's alright" but you never get enthusiastic feedback. Recently, though, Charles [Thompson, lead singer of the Pixies] talked about when he first saw the artwork with the man with the hairy back. He packed in his job that day saying "I knew then we had a band." Rather a marvellous thing to say.'
Vaughan Oliver

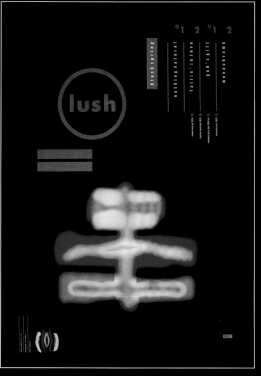

Above left
Lush *Black Spring* promotional
poster [Art direction and design:
Vaughan Oliver; photography:
Jim Friedman],
October 1991

Above right
13 Year Itch poster for 4AD
festival at the ICA
[Art direction and design:
Vaughan Oliver; photography:
Tony Gibson],
July 1993

Above left
Pixies 'Velouria' single
promotional poster
[Art direction and design:
Vaughan Oliver; photography:
Simon Larbalestier],
July 1990

Below left
His Name Is Alive *Livonia*
promotional poster
[Art direction and design:
Vaughan Oliver; photography:
Beverley Carruthers],
June 1990

Above right
Pixies *Bossanova* promotional
poster [Art direction and design:
Vaughan Oliver; photography:
Simon Larbalestier],
August 1990

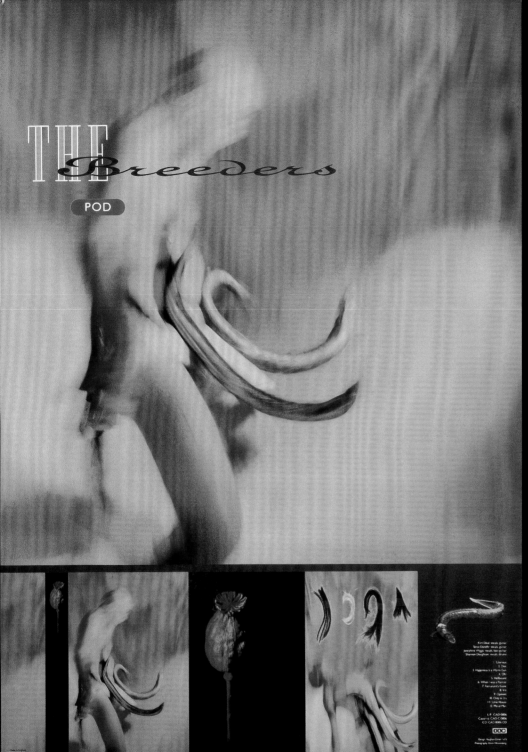

Top right
Gus Gus *Polydistortion*
promotional poster
[Art direction and design:
Vaughan Oliver; photography:
Chris Biggs],
April 1997

Above left
The Breeders *Pod* promotional
poster [Art direction and design:
Vaughan Oliver; photography:
Kevin Westerberg],
May 1990

Above right
Colourbox *Colourbox* CAD508
promotional poster [Art direction
and design: Vaughan Oliver;
photography: Chris Biggs],
August 1985

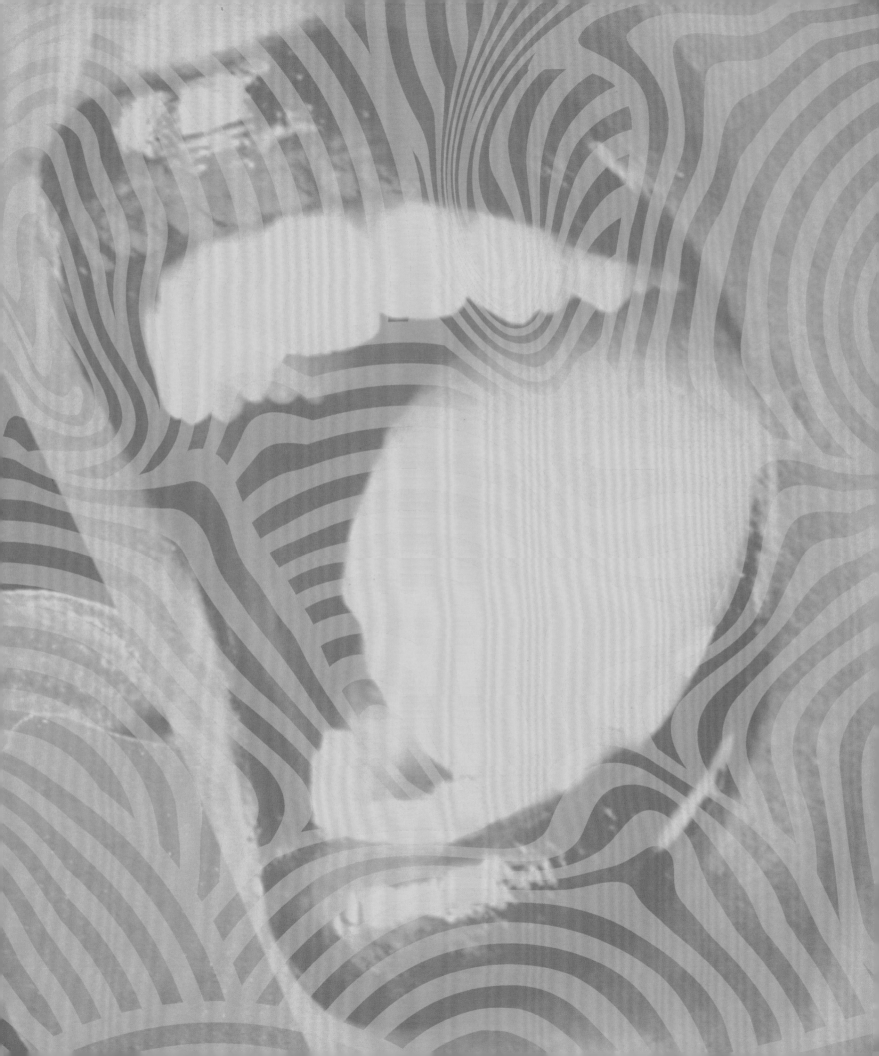

01

CLUB, DANCE &RAVE

TECHNO-GRAPHIC

In the late 1980s, a whole new dance-oriented pop culture developed that centred itself on vast club venues and open-air 'raves'. These events were driven by new forms of electronic dance music, including acid house, techno, electronica and trance, which were often enjoyed in conjunction with a new party drug, Ecstasy.

The phenomenon initially took off in clubs and warehouse parties in and around Manchester and London. Known as 'acid house parties', these (often illegal) gatherings were soon dubbed 'raves' by the media, and a new teen subculture was born. Borrowing from punk's 'do-it-yourself' ethos to organize the events, rave culture soon developed its own graphic style, with purpose-made flyers to suit each occasion.

Although most of the raves and club nights resembled latter-day discotheques, with DJs taking centre stage, new rock acts emerged as part of the club scene – particularly in Manchester, where Factory Records were the pioneers of the new 'Madchester' music, and forged an iconic visual style to match.

To fill the dearth of clubbing hot spots in Manchester, Factory's Tony Wilson set up 'Madchester's' spiritual home, the infamous Haçienda nightclub, which featured house music, raves, DJs and local bands, including the Happy Mondays. Despite being one of the best-known clubs in the world, the Haçienda ran at a loss, largely due to the low sales of alcohol (the punters preferred Ecstasy and water), and was kept afloat primarily by New Order's record sales.

During the early nineties computers flooded onto the scene, and artworks soon reflected the widespread availability of new software programs, employing overt displays of technical complexity and incorporating elaborate digital patterns and textures only made possible by the new technology. At the same time, inspired by the DJ-driven dance culture, 'sampling' in music became widely used and accepted. This was soon reflected in the work of the designers, who would plunder disparate graphic styles and references in a visual version of the sampling process.

In the record industry there was a shift of emphasis from live performance to recorded product and, correspondingly, recordings were released that would increasingly have been difficult to reproduce live on stage. As a result, touring by live acts declined, particularly on the club circuit and, as a consequence, tour posters also became more scarce.

Central Station Design, who worked closely with the Happy Mondays among others, found themselves at the epicenter of the Manchester movement. Their designs created a unique visual language using hand-drawn letter forms, new typographical styles, collage, screen-print, paint and new technology, and their work was the antithesis of the post-punk obsession with Futurism, Bauhaus and the Swiss euro typographical style. Tony Wilson comments: 'The second half of the Factory story is best summed up by the painterly eccentricity of Central Station, Matt, Pat and Karen.'

Above left
Happy Mondays *Pills 'n' Thrills and Bellyaches* promotional poster [Central Station Design], November 1990

Above right
Happy Mondays *Bummed* promotional poster [Central Station Design], November 1988

Inspired by the culturally and musically
diverse scene at London warehouse
parties, Trevor Jackson began his own
design label, Bite It!, in 1987. Jackson's
artwork style reveals an almost cautious
approach to colour, often focussing on
just one or two colours and a range of
contrasting fonts (he regularly returns
to black and white designs). Says
Jackson: 'I aim to make strong and
simple results that, most importantly,
solve a brief.' His career has seen him
produce music remixes and he has
formed his own Output Record label.
The above posters are examples of his
early, much imitated, artworks.

ARE YOU TOUGH ENOUGH FOR

TACK»HEAD

Starting out as the unofficial house band for Sugarhill Records, Tackhead were formed with the addition of dub genius Adrian Sherwood. Their music combined diverse genres, including dance, rock and dub, to create a unique sound that was to prove influential for years to come. The Me Company artwork featured on this page echoes the political cut-up style that the band employed at times.

Above left
Tackhead sticker
[Design: Me Company;
Art direction: Paul White;
Logo design: Jill Mumford],
1989

Above right, centre and below
Tackhead illustrations;
alternative designs
[Design: Me Company;
Art direction: Paul White],
1989

PETER SAVILLE

Alongside his friend Malcolm Garrett, Peter Saville turned rock design on its head in the wake of punk in the late 1970s, bringing a consciously Modernist approach to bear in his work for the new wave of clubs and bands based in Manchester.

Born in the Manchester suburb of Hale in 1955, Saville met Garrett at grammar school, where both were introduced to graphic design by their art teacher, Peter Hancock. In 1974 Saville went on to study graphics at Manchester Polytechnic, while Garrett spent a year on the graphic design course at Reading University. Although the latter only lasted a year 'down south', Saville reckons it was crucial to their mutual development: 'A fundamental influence on the imagery of pop was Malcolm Garrett's year at Reading University. It was the only University in Britain that actually had a graphic design course at the time, so Malcolm gave it a try. He discovered after one term that he didn't enjoy it, he found it incredibly dry and academic, and in comparison with my experience at Manchester Polytechnic, a bit too dull. So Malcolm completed his first year at Reading, and then joined up again with me at Manchester Polytechnic for three years, on the Graphic degree course. But the year that Malcolm had at Reading, and the information that was opened up to him, and in particular the reading list, came to constitute almost a tipping point in the imagery and identity of British pop.'

The catalyst for Saville was a book from that reading list, which Garrett showed him after he'd moved back to Manchester. It was titled *Pioneers of Modern Typography:* 'They had that book in the library at Manchester Polytechnic, but no one talked about it. In the curriculum of graphics in seventies art colleges, the history of graphic design and its relationship to Modernism was not on the agenda.' What Saville saw as lacking in the 'pop art' approach to graphics that began in America in the sixties – which he describes as 'the New York School of Visual Wit' – was very apparent in music visuals. 'Prior to the late seventies, pop – whether it's record covers or posters – was not "designed". There is a sensibility pertaining to typographic order and layout, that begins to influence and define the work. That's not to say there weren't beautifully crafted works before the late seventies, but they are not really about "design". There were some great artists, great designers, doing beautiful work, some with an innate sense of composition

While they were still at the polytechnic, punk arrived and changed the pop culture landscape forever. There were new bands, new venues and new record companies. Saville and Garrett decided the scene could do with some new graphics – Garrett famously working for local band the Buzzcocks, Saville as co-founder of the fledgling Factory Records, set up by local TV journalist-come-pop entrepreneur Tony Wilson. 'Malcolm's background had been sort of Captain Beefheart and Frank Zappa, and mine had been from David Bowie to Roxy Music, and we had a common ground in Kraftwerk. The first album that I went and bought for myself was Kraftwerk's *Autobahn*, and in the UK in the early seventies the album cover had the German autobahn sign, the motorway sign, and that had a profound effect on me. My first piece of work at Factory was a poster, "Fac 1" – the one that has a hearing protection sign on it – that's basically my version of the autobahn sign'.

That initial poster was for Wilson's club night called Factory, before he launched the record label in 1979 with Saville as art director. With Factory Records Saville designed memorable graphics for bands including Joy Division and New Order, which came to define the new wave of Manchester music in the eighties. Likewise, when Factory opened the Haçienda club in 1982, Saville provided the trademark visual images in its identity.

In one classic Factory Records moment, a Saville-designed New Order programme showed up somewhat late, as New Order drummer Stephen Morris explains: 'It was the programme he did for us on an American tour that turned up on the last gig, and we've still got thousands rotting away in a warehouse somewhere that we can't get rid of.' Saville went on to be hugely in demand in the pop mainstream as fashion caught up with art, with work for bands as diverse as Wham!, Roxy Music and Ultravox, before more recently diversifying into corporate design and fashion.

But it was in his work for the then-radical Factory that his committed brand of technically sophisticated Modernism impacted on the British rock scene, an irony that's not lost on him now, as Creative Director for the City of Manchester: 'The authorities closed down all of the venues for new music in Manchester in 1977, which is why Tony (Wilson) took it upon himself to start a club night called the Factory, and then you end up a quarter century later sitting in

'In many ways it was the tyranny of promoters, who just wanted the band's name and dates in day-glo, that limited the potential of music poster design – it was not until you got the kind of self-determination, as epitomized by the Haçienda, that there was a conscious control of communication.'
Peter Saville

FAC–2

A FACTORY SAMPLE

Above
'A Factory Sample' EP cover
[Peter Saville],

Opposite
The Factory, Manchester
[Peter Saville],

USE HEARING PROTECTION

MAY 19-THE DURUTTI COLUMN/JILTED JOHN

MAY 26-BIG IN JAPAN/MANICURED NOISE

THE FACTORY

JUNE 2-THE DURRUTTI COLUMN/CABARET VOLTAIRE

JUNE 9-THE TILLER BOYS/JOY DIVISION

RUSSEL CLUB   ROYCE RD   MOSS SIDE

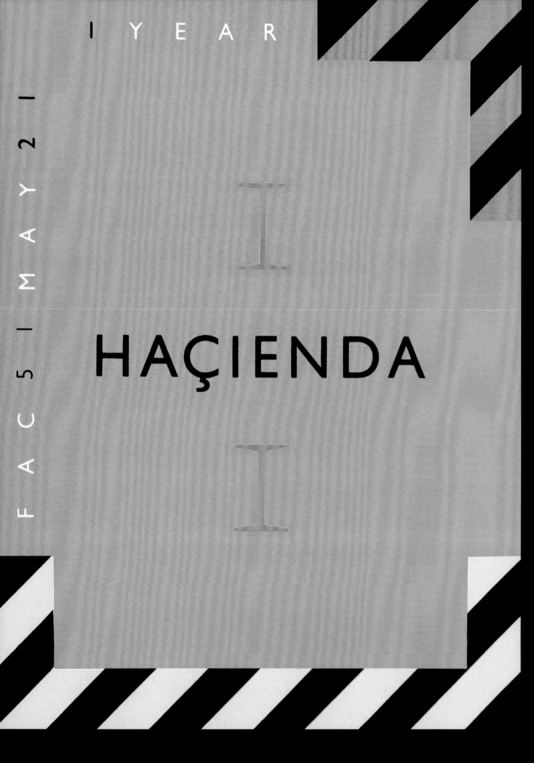

F A C 5 I M A Y 2 I

I Y E A R

HAÇIENDA

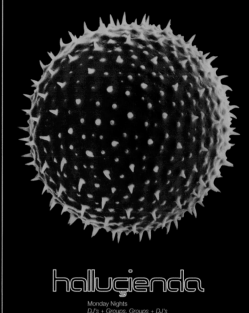

halluçienda
Monday Nights
DJ's + Groups, Groups + DJ's

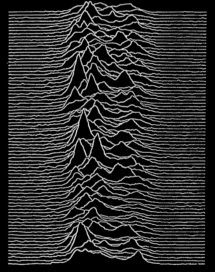

FACT 10 + 4 –FACTORY RECORDS

JUNE '79

FACT 10	–**UNKNOWN PLEASURES** The first album by Joy Division.
FAC 5	–**ALL NIGHT PARTY** Single by A Certain Ratio.
FAC 6	–**ELECTRICITY** Single by Orchestral Manoeuvres in the Dark.

JULY '79

FAC 11	–**ENGLISH BLACK BOYS** Single by X-O-Dus.
FAC 12	–**TIME GOES BY SO SLOW** Single by The Distractions.

Above left
Haçienda poster [Peter Saville],
May 1983

Above right
Haçienda 'Halluçienda' poster
[Peter Saville],
1989

Above left
Spectrum 'Theatre of Madness'
flyer,
April 1988

Right, clockwise from top left
Helter Skelter '20th Century Rox'
flyer [Steve Perry a.k.a. Pez],
December 1999

Helter Skelter 'Lost in Music'
flyer [Steve Perry a.k.a. Pez],
March 1999

Warehouse party flyer,
Blackburn,
1989

Warehouse party flyer, London,
April 1989

Warehouse 'Truth' flyer,
Plymouth ['Me'],
April 1993

'Blast' flyer, Blackpool,
July 1995

With the increased popularity of
warehouse parties, promoters began to
produce their own flyers, employing the
same home-made principles as punk.
With venues constantly under threat
of being raided by the police for illegal
entry, the addresses were often hastily
added at the last minute so as to allow
for any changes.

For the Z-shed flyer, designer Ben Pearson was inspired by a press ad: 'The ad showed a guy spraying on some deodorant and instead of mist, multi-coloured stripes were coming out of the can. I'd already decided I wanted to do something involving vomit and from there I just experimented.' Pearson says he approaches design using a cut-and-paste mentality, rather than relying on computers: 'For me, the acid test is whether or not my design would sit comfortably next to one of the old punk posters from the early eighties.'

For the flyer advertising the Feline club night (below right) at Herbal in East London, which featured all-female performers, Ria Dastidar incorporated vibrant-pink versions of the female gender symbol in her artwork: 'I tend to mix everything up, then infuse it with colour and, hopefully, a bit of chaos.'

Above left
Z-shed flyer, Corsica Studios, London [Rachel Goldstein and Ben Pearson],
June 2007

Above right
Lovebox London Weekender afterparty flyer,
July 2007

Below right
Feline flyer, Herbal club, London [Ria Dastidar],
Winter 2006, Spring 2007

DRUM & BASS
ARENA PRESENT
THE BATTLE ARENA
FRIDAY 11 MARCH
AT THE END

DJS
ZINC B2B FRICTION
PENDULUM B2B
SIMON 'BASSLINE' SMITH
CLIPZ B2B BARON
TK B2B UTAH JAZZ

MCS
DYNAMITE
EKSMAN B2B HERBZIE
E-LL
BIGGIE

FRIDAY 11 MARCH AT THE END
WEST CENTRAL ST / LONDON
/10PM-6.00AM
£11 ADVANCE / £13 DOOR
TICKET HOTLINE: 08700 600100 OR BUY ONLINE
AT: WWW.BREAKBEAT.CO.UK/TICKETWEB

AKA

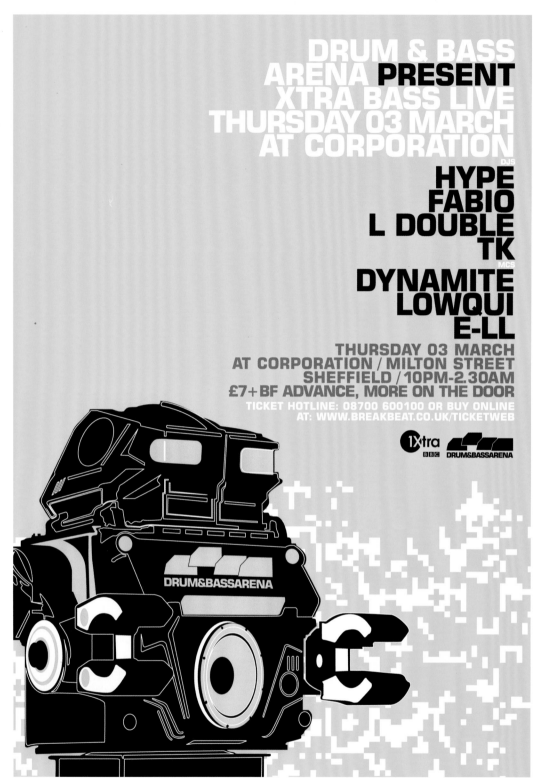

DRUM & BASS
ARENA PRESENT
XTRA BASS LIVE
THURSDAY 03 MARCH
AT CORPORATION

DJS
HYPE
FABIO
L DOUBLE
TK

MCS
DYNAMITE
LOWQUI
E-LL

THURSDAY 03 MARCH
AT CORPORATION / MILTON STREET
SHEFFIELD / 10PM-2.30AM
£7 + BF ADVANCE, MORE ON THE DOOR

TICKET HOTLINE: 08700 600100 OR BUY ONLINE
AT: WWW.BREAKBEAT.CO.UK/TICKETWEB

1Xtra
BBC DRUM&BASSARENA

DRUM&BASSARENA

DRUM AND
BASS ARENA
PRESENTS
XTRA BASS
LIVE ON 1X

DJ RAP
MAMPI SWIFT
BRYAN GEE
SHY FX
MC SKIBADEE
ECHER & BLITZ
MC JUNIOR RED
& TONN PIPER

During the nineties, dance music was played onstage using the newly affordable technologies of synthesizers, sequencers, samples and drum loops. Live performances were augmented by elaborate projected backdrops to make up for the sometimes static performances onstage (after all, people came to dance and lose themselves in the music, not watch a DJ 'perform'). With the musical artists often taking a role more akin to a producer or engineer, many chose to remain anonymous, leaving the artwork designers free to interpret the music in any way they saw fit.

The designs for Drum & Bass Arena, illustrated here, were created by Daniel Koch of London-based Zip Design. The flyers include the motif of a classic toy robot fused with a sound system (synonymous of drum and bass music), while the colour palette echoes the strong yellow and black of the Drum & Bass Arena logo.

Above left
Corporation, Sheffield
[Daniel Koch],
March 2006

Above right
The End Club, London
[Daniel Koch],
March 2005

Below right
Drum & Bass Arena flyers
[Daniel Koch]
March 2005

Ali Augur's flyers for Plastic People events featured drawings of famous London music sites, while stripping all the words and logos from the buildings and placing the dancing Plastic People logo in their place. Above and below are his takes on the Rainbow Theatre and the Astoria in Charing Cross Road. Augur said of his work for Plastic People: '"The big idea", "Keep it simple" and "Three's a campaign" are all rules that I had started to adopt in my work. Rules which, when applied to the humble club flyer, make for powerful work. I was fortunate enough to be introduced to a club and its owner in 1998 that would allow me to test these rules and play out my ideas.'

The flyer by Russell Reid promoted an Easter Sunday event for the Liverpool club night, Circus, whose 'ring leader' is Radio 1 DJ, Yousef. It was part of a series in which Reid was experimenting with merging elements from nature with human features; the result, in Reid's own words, 'felt energetic and bizarre.'

PLAN B

JANUARY 2010 HIGHLIGHTS

BASEMENT JAXX (DJ SET)
BROOKES BROTHERS
FABIO
▶FALTYDL
JAMIE VEX'D
JEHST
MARTYN
ROSKA
SOLO
2562

WWW.PLANB-LONDON.COM
418 BRIXTON ROAD, LONDON SW9

PLAN B
SATURDAY 30TH JANUARY

BASEMENT JAXX

WWW.PLANB-LONDON.COM

With the advent of affordable home studio programs and more powerful personal computers, DJs more recently have been able to compose music at home, and electronic dance music has witnessed a resurgence. Designer Kate Moross, who runs her own label, ISO, designs flyers for many of these club nights. Moross scans in or photographs her drawings and then uses Illustrator and Photoshop to perfect the design. Her fondness for creating her own typefaces and the need to show a long list of names have led to some memorable designs: 'I have a fascination with three-sided shapes, illegible typography and free-form lettering.'

Above left
Plan B flyer, London
[Kate Moross],
January 2010

Above right
Plan B flyer, London
[Kate Moross/Jack
Featherstone],
January 2010

Below right
Mucha Marcha club night
flyer [Kate Moross],
August 2007

TEAMS:

ORGASMIC CUISINE

CHROMAIN ROCK

QUEENS OF NOISE

GUCCI SOUND SYSTEM

WoWoW

MATTHEW SLATER GT

REJOCUISINIEL

FABRIC MYSTERY

VICE MAGAZINE

PEOPLE ARE GERMS

FLYPLAY

DJ SET:
THE BROKEN HEARTS

BETHNAL GREEN
WORKING MEN'S CLUB
42 POLLARD ROW
LONDON E2 6NB

MORE INFO ON:
WWW.MYSPACE.COM/OFFICIALUKIPODBATTLE
FLYER BY KATEMOROSS.COM

TEST CARD

LIVE LIVE
Apache Beat
Frankmusik
Tacteel
(TTC/instubes)
DJSET DJSET
Lou and Nova

HOXTON BAR AND KITCHEN
18TH OCTOBER
£5 IN ADVANCE

KATE MOROSS

CHROMATICS

Above left
iPod Battle, London event
poster [Kate Moross],
March 2007

Above right
Chromatics, Café 1001 flyer,
London [Kate Moross],
April 2008

Below left
Test Card club night flyer
[Kate Moross],
October 2009

NEED2SOUL
SATURDAY
28TH FEBRUARY
AT CARGO
MOODYMANN
(DET.RIOT)
BENJI B (XTRA)
LIAMSKI & ISA
(ALL ENDS UP)
SPECIAL AUDIO
VISUAL
SCREENING
AT 9.30 PM

Need2Soul
Saturday 28th february
At cargo
Moodymann (Detroit/Mahogani Music)
Benji B (xtra/Deviation)
Liamski & Isa (All Ends Up)
special Audio visual screening at 9.30 Pm
–
£6 before 9pm
£10 after
£10 in adv from
www.ticketweb.co.uk
8pm–3am
–
Cargo,
83 rivington st
kingsland viaduct
shoreditch
london EC2A 3AY
–
www.cargo-london.com
www.need2soul.com
www.iwantdesign.co.uk

NEED2SOUL
SATURDAY
18TH JULY
THEO
PARRISH
(SOUND
SIGNATURE/
DETROIT)
JIM LISTER
& KERRY JEAN
POWER (FEEL UP)
LUCA C (KITSUNE)

–
NEED 2 SOUL
Saturday
18th July
–

THEO
PARISH
(Sound Signature/Detroit)
Jim Lister & Kerry Jean Power
(Feel Up)
Luca C (Kitsune

10.00pm – 5.00am
Bar A Bar
135 Stoke Newington High St N16
£12 From www.ticketweb.co.uk
–
www.need2soul.co.uk
www.iwantdesign.co.uk
–

FERTILIZER
FESTIVAL
.COM

fertilizer
GOOD SHIT FROM POLAND
Rich Mix / Cargo / Hoxton Hall
12–17MAY 2009
SING SING
PENELOPE
JACASZEK
CONTEMPORARY
NOISE SEXTET
PINK FREUD
& PETE WAREHAM
MAŁE INSTRUMENTY
FISZ
MITCH & MITCH
BAABA

The finest new music from Poland
today / Underground sounds that
fertilize the mainstream / From
electronica, postrock psychedlia,
hip hop and jazz to an orchestra of
toy instruments / Sound postcards
and Polish film-making at its best

Produced by
the :: hub   sounduk   POLSKA! YEAR   RICH/MIX

design: iwantdesign.co.uk

Above left
Need 2 Soul/Cargo promotional
poster, London [iwant],
February 2009

Below left
Need 2 Soul/Bar A Bar
promotional poster, London
[iwant],
July 2009

Above right
Fertilizer Festival poster, London
[iwant],
May 2009

With the advent of digital tools such as Photoshop, designers became free to manipulate the shape and form of typography without restriction. Many designers started to experiment with the shapes made by the letters themselves, distilling them down to their basic components, and then rebuilding them into exciting images (some more legible than others). iwant design's John Gilsenan uses hand lettering and cut-up collages to create lush typographic landscapes, which appeal to a design-savvy audience. With a broad client base, iwant's work has included the surrealist-influenced album promotion for Hungarian band the Unbending Trees.

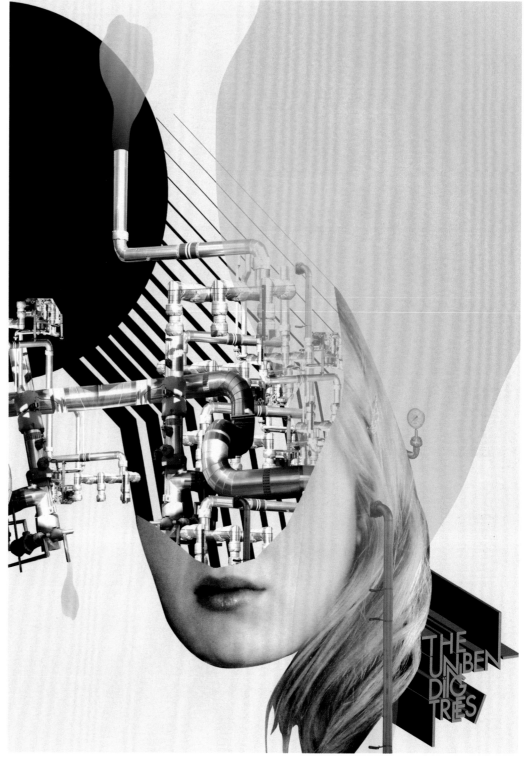

Above left
Buzzin Fly, Cardiff [iwant],
June 2009

Above right
Unbending Trees *Chemically Happy (Is the New Sad)* promotional poster [iwant],
October 2008

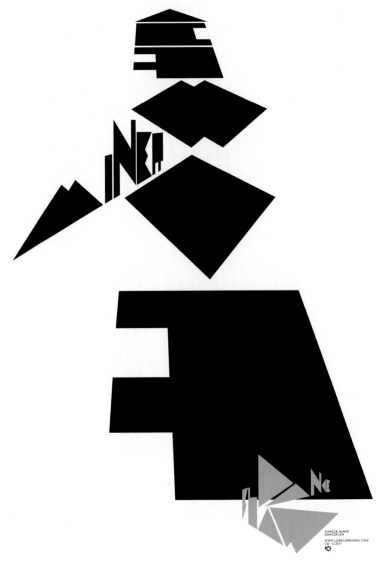

Design team Non-Format look at ways to break the traditional rules of typography. In the posters featured on this page and opposite, they have removed the 'keys' (spaces) from the letters, made them super-bold, and then – as in the examples above – distorted them on different planes of perspective. Their experimental approach has led to numerous commissions from global brands such as Nike and O2.

Above left
The Vowels *Pattern Prism*
promotional poster
[Non-Format],
September 2009

Above right
Cursor Miner *Danceflaw*
promotional poster
[Non-Format],
May 2006

ART
ART
ART
DON'T
MAKE
NO
RAVE
DAVE.

THE CHAP
MEGA BREAKFAST
LORECORDINGS.COM

PROPER
SONGS
ABOUT
GIRLS
AND
CLUBBING.

THE CHAP
MEGA BREAKFAST
NEW ALBUM OUT NOW
LORECORDINGS.COM

MASSIVE
TUNES.
PUT
THEM
ON
YOUR
POD
POD.

THE CHAP
MEGA BREAKFAST
LORECORDINGS.COM

HATCHBACK
colors of the sun

out now on lo recordings
for a free track from this album:
www.lorecordings.com/free

Above, left to right
The Chap *Megabreakfast*
promotional posters
[Non-Format],
July 2008

Below right
Hatchback *Colors of the Sun*
promotional poster
[Non-Format],
September 2008

ACOLYTE

THE ALBUM

DELPHIC

Non-Format's impressive cover for the 12-inch vinyl release of the 2010 album by Delphic, *Acolyte* – described by Simon Price of the *Independent* as 'on kissing terms with magnificence' – featured a striking photographic image. Non-Format's Jon Forss explains: 'When the type work is combined with new photographic elements, themselves the result of many hours of experimenting in a photo studio, the results are incredibly rewarding.'

Above
Delphic *Acolyte* album cover
[Non-Format and Jake Walters],
January 2010

The Big Chill festival has grown steadily in popularity since its first outdoor event in 1995. This playful brand and poster design was created by London agency, bleach, who approached a selection of 32 illustrators to illuminate a quotation in their own individual styles, resulting in a series of posters as different from each other as the music on offer at the festival.

STATE OF THE ART

CONTEMPORARY IMAGES

Moving into the 21st century, British rock art has become as diverse as the music it represents. Previously, music and the artwork it generated could fairly easily be attributed to a particular decade. It could safely be said, for example, that the late sixties was the era of psychedelic music and psychedelic posters, and the late seventies that of punk music and punk graphics. Now, no single musical style holds sway; no particular genre is dominant in the age of the digital download. Similarly, rock poster design ranges from the plainly retro to cutting-edge high-tech, with innumerable variations in between.

As computer technology has become universally available, designers have grown increasingly wary of a perceived vacuity of content and a consequent devaluation of basic design skills. The answer, for many artists, has been to marry traditional illustration techniques with those of computer programs, and in so doing to create new, previously technically impossible, styles. Major design studios, such as iwant and Non-Format (a British-Norwegian company until recently based in the UK), now cater for bands and record companies as part of a far wider portfolio of commercial and corporate clients, while the bulk of contemporary rock posters are produced by designers either working on their own or as part of local, loose-knit collectives. Contact with similar groups in the US has also led to the recent phenomenon of American designers creating works for British bands and venues.

With this proliferation of creative sources, poster-led British rock art shows no sign of declining. And with record sales plummeting in the face of internet downloads, the focus for bands has turned once again to live performance. The vast majority of groups are now making their largest profits from touring, which, not so long ago, was considered a loss-making exercise staged to promote the latest album. Consequently, concert posters have made a reappearance despite the declining CD market – representing a genuine renaissance in the art of British rock as we move into the second decade of the century.

xendless_xurbia

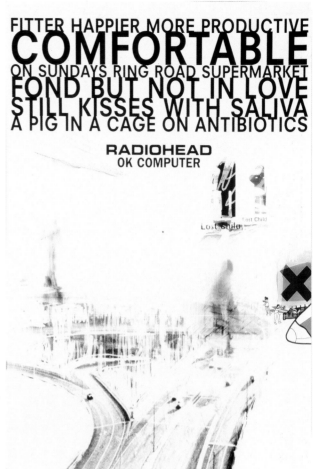

FITTER HAPPIER MORE PRODUCTIVE
COMFORTABLE
ON SUNDAYS RING ROAD SUPERMARKET
FOND BUT NOT IN LOVE
STILL KISSES WITH SALIVA
A PIG IN A CAGE ON ANTIBIOTICS

RADIOHEAD
OK COMPUTER

MUSE

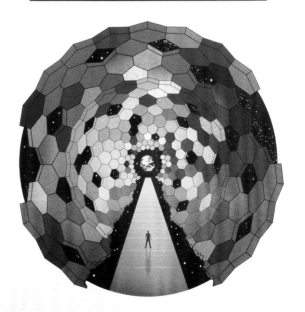

THE RESISTANCE

'Xendless Xurbia' was a virtual 'label' created by Radiohead when they put out *In Rainbows* as an internet-only download release in 2007. The artwork was by Stanley Donwood (a.k.a Dan Rickwood), who has been the band's 'in-house' designer since their album *The Bends* in 1995.

The art for Muse's album *The Resistance* was the work of London-based company La Boca, who describe themselves as 'an independent design circus specializing in art and design for the film, music and fashion industries'.

Above left
Radiohead *Xendless Xurbia* poster [Stanley Donwood], October 2007

Above right
Radiohead *OK Computer* promotional poster, June 1997

Below right
Muse *The Resistance* promotional poster [La Boca], September 2009

ANGEL
MASSIVE ATTACK 13.7.98
THE NEW SINGLE ON CD.12″. MC FEATURES REMIXES FROM BLUR & MAD PROFESSOR

Left
Massive Attack 'Angel'

Opposite, top
Massive Attack 'Mezzanine'

Opposite, below left
Massive Attack 'Inertia Creeps'

Opposite, below right
Massive Attack 'Tear Drop'

All images
Massive Attack campaign posters [Art direction and design: Tom Hingston Studio and Robert Del Naja; photography: Nick Knight], 1998–1999

MASSIVE ATTACK
MEZZANINE 20.4.98

Established in 1997, Tom Hingston Studio is a London-based multi-disciplinary design agency working across a range of fields, including fashion, film, advertising, branding and music. Their clients include the Rolling Stones, Nick Cave and Robbie Williams. Featured on this spread are posters for Massive Attack's *Mezzanine* album campaign. The use of a sans serif typeface, coupled with the dark and beautiful image of the stag beetle, creates a resonating visual. The entomological vibe was carried through all of the subsequent promotional material for the album's singles.

MASSIVE ATTACK
INERTIA CREEPS

TEAR DROP
MASSIVE ATTACK 27.4.98
CD.12". MC FEATURES REMIXES FROM PRIMAL SCREAM & MAD PROFESSOR

100TH WINDOW

MASSIVE ATTACK

CD/LP 10/02/03

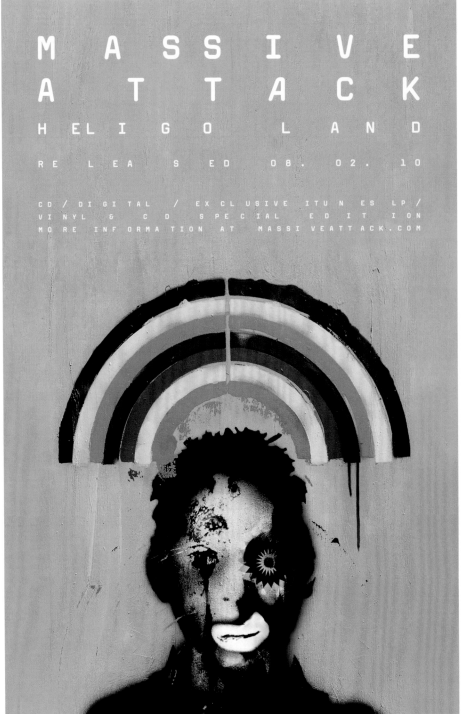

M A S S I V E
A T T A C K
H E L I G O L A N D
R E L E A S E D   0 8 .   0 2 .   1 0

C D / D I G I TAL / EX CL USIVE ITU N ES LP /
VI NYL & C D S PECIAL ED IT ION
MO RE INFOR MATION AT MASSI VEATTACK.COM

Massive Attack's *Heligoland* hit the national newspapers when London Underground banned the poster promoting the album from all its stations, because they felt it looked too much like graffiti. 'They won't allow anything on the Tube that looks like street art,' band member Robert '3D' Del Naja told the *Daily Star*. 'They want us to remove all drips and fuzz. It's the most absurd censorship I've ever seen.'

Above left
Massive Attack *100th Window*
[Art direction and design: Tom Hingston Studio and Robert Del Naja; photography: Nick Knight],
February 2003

Above right
Massive Attack *Heligoland*
[Art direction and design: Tom Hingston Studio; art: Robert Del Naja],
February 2010

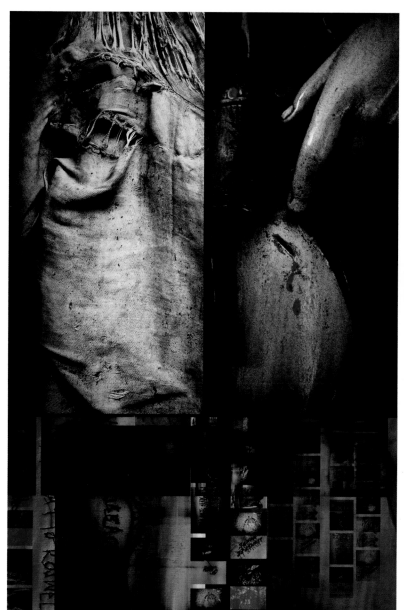

Says Charles Thompson (a.k.a. Frank Black), lead singer with the Pixies, of their epic box set *Minotaur*, 'We realize we have a unique relationship with Vaughan. He's the only person outside of the band who has ever been allowed to represent the band in any way, and we've given him carte blanche to do that.' As well as containing all of the Pixies' studio albums produced on 24-carat gold-plated CDs, Oliver designed a 54-page book to go into the custom container. A group of art students, taught by Oliver at the University of Creative Arts in Epsom, were selected to help create the different parts of the packaging.

Above left and right
Pixies *Minotaur* box set
promotional posters
[Art direction and design:
Vaughan Oliver; photography:
Simon Larbalestier],
November 2009

FESTIVALS

Today, large-scale UK rock festivals such as Reading and Glastonbury have achieved the status of national institution. With corporate sponsorship, live television coverage and slick organization, they are very much part of the music industry establishment. And yet during what many consider to have been the 'golden age' of the rock festival – the late sixties and early seventies – such gatherings were seen as an expression of the counterculture, for which rock music provided the soundtrack.

The roots of British open-air music events can be traced back to the late 1950s, when the annual festival organized by the National Jazz Federation was first staged. As more blues and then rock 'n' roll acts became involved, the event – staged at Richmond, in Surrey, and later Windsor, Berkshire – became the Jazz and Blues Festival, then the Jazz Blues and Rock Festival, and eventually evolved into the Reading Festival that we know today.

Glastonbury, now a mainstream event attracting people from all walks of life, started out in 1971 as part of the hippy-oriented alternative rock scene, and for a number of years was regarded as the UK inheritor of the 'spirit of Woodstock'. Likewise, the three Isle of Wight festivals from 1968 to 1970 – the last two events drawing enormous crowds of up to a quarter of a million visitors – were seen as a cipher for the new culture of youth.

The challenge for the graphic imagery at such huge, multi-act presentations has been to present a good deal of information while retaining a style reflecting the spirit of the event. At heavy metal extravaganzas, such as Monsters of Rock and the Download Festival, bands often provided their own logos, so the posters 'designed themselves', with the plethora of images and typefaces from the various acts.

Having to deal with an excess of information – from a design point of view – was a particular issue in the era of the psychedelic poster, when the swirling graphics and day-glo colours often rendered the simplest of messages virtually unreadable. The solution at the Isle of Wight events was to have a consistent image – in 1969 it was the art deco-style King Kong figure; in 1970 it was a moustached drummer – running above the informative text on posters, flyers and tickets. In this way, the event acquired a strong graphic image of its own, over and above that of any of the bands taking part.

The Bath Festival of Blues encountered a similar problem. A lower-key event than the Isle of Wight, in 1969 there were 19 acts, plus DJ John Peel, all appearing between noon and 11pm, and all of whom had to be named on the hand-drawn poster. In the end, a psychedelic illustration combined with an easy-to-read 'flower power' font solved the problem. The same style, but without any illustration, was adopted the following year for the two-day Bath Festival of Blues and Progressive Music, as it was now called.

In recent years, as the big festivals have become more corporate and homogenized, so, too, has much of the associated publicity material. Arguably, more interesting artworks can be seen at the lower-key, independently promoted festivals – music weekends like the locally sponsored GuilFest in Guildford, Surrey, and the December two-day Nightmare Before Christmas in Minehead, Somerset.

'The great pop festivals of the late 1960s were very much a product of their times – youthful rebellion, music as popular art, a derangement of all the senses – but their underlying search for shared freedom and community had deep cultural roots.'
Brian Hinton, *Message To Love: The Isle of Wight Festivals 1968–70* (Castle Communications, 1995)

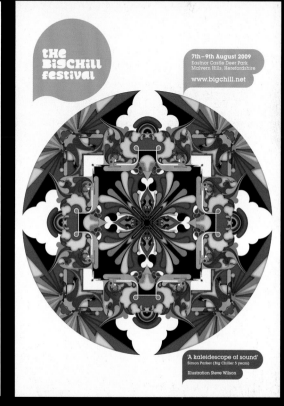

Above left
Isle of Wight Festival of Music
ticket [Dave Roe],
August 1969

Above right
Nightmare Before Christmas
poster [Tim Biskup],
December 2009

Below left
Bath Festival of Blues,
June 1969

Below right
The Big Chill poster
[Design: bleach; illustration:
Steve Wilson],
August 2009

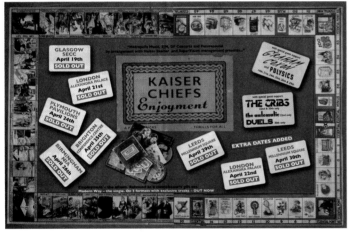

The Kaiser Chiefs enlisted the talents of Cally Calloman at Antar for their debut album *Employment*, the design of which was in the form of a retro board game. The Antar design company have been responsible for a number of the band's album and single covers.

Franz Ferdinand's drummer, Paul Thompson, created the band's iconic graphics, including the image shown above right, which he appropriated from a famous 1924 poster design by the Russian Constructivist artist Alexander Rodchenko.

Above and below left
Kaiser Chiefs *Employment*
poster and packaging
[Cally Calloman],
March 2005

Above right
Franz Ferdinand *You Could Have It So Much Better*
promotional poster
[Paul Thompson],
October 2005

Virtual band Gorillaz was the twin inspiration of their founders, Blur front man Damon Albarn and the cartoon artist Jamie Hewlett, otherwise known for his creation of the *Tank Girl* comic book series. The animated Gorillaz band members, 2D, Murdoc Niccals, Noodle and Russell Hobbs, were all designed by Hewlett, and are now as familiar as most 'real' bands on the scene, with their image ubiquitous on albums, posters and T-shirts.

Right
Gorillaz *Speed Pigeon* poster
[Jamie Hewlett],
2001

Left
Arctic Monkeys, The Faversham,
Leeds [Matt Ferres],
June 2005

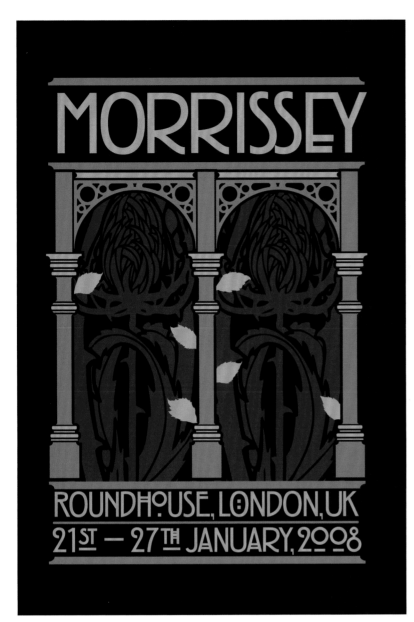

The Faversham (opposite) is a multi-purpose venue on the edge of Leeds city centre which functions as a restaurant by day, a bar by night, and a nightclub into the early hours of the morning. The place has featured some of the biggest names around since the mid-2000s, including Franz Ferdinand, Lily Allen, the Fratellis and the Arctic Monkeys – whose poster here was created by one of the venue's regular designers, Matt Ferres.

Creative consultancy Stylorouge have been designing for advertising, film, television and – their speciality – the music business, since the early 1980s. Recent work includes the 2008 poster, shown left, for a Morrissey appearance at the Roundhouse, and the catalogue for the 'Sound & Vision' Cancer Research fundraiser auction, held at the legendary EMI studios in Abbey Road.

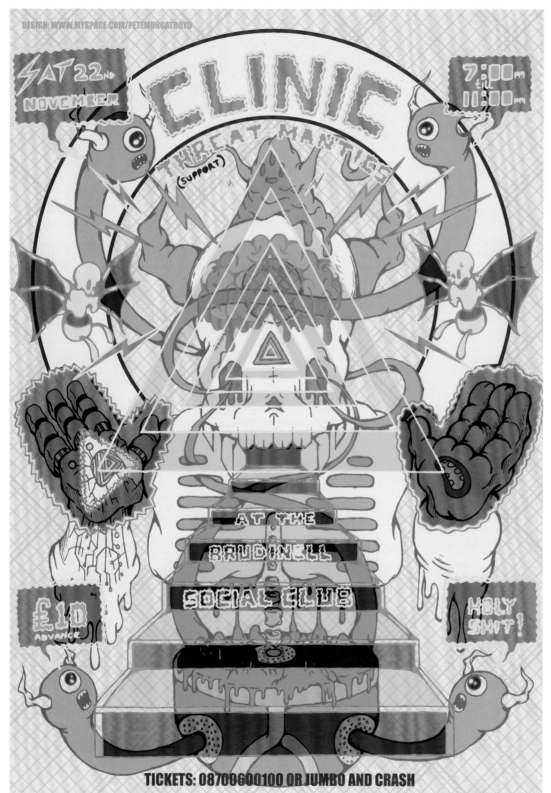

Above left
Brudenell Social Club, Leeds
[Pete Murgatroyd],
November 2008

Above right
The Library, Leeds
[Pete Murgatroyd],
September 2009

Below right
Brudenell Social Club, Leeds
[Pete Murgatroyd],
July 2009

Since graduating from Leeds
Metropolitan University in 2004,
Pete Murgatroyd has been developing
a design style which he describes
as 'heavily influenced by B-movies,
monster schlock and comic books.'
Using a technique involving multiple
hand-drawn layers, he produces
posters, fanzine covers and
merchandise for local bands, venues
(in particular the Brudenell Social
Club), and new record labels, including
the Leeds-based Brew Records.

'I've always drawn things,' says Tom J. Newell, who created all the posters on this page. After studying Fine Art in Sheffield, Newell spent three months travelling around France with his band, during which time he 'drew some wacky, decorative posters to promote our gigs'. After returning to England, Newell moved to London, where he has worked on gig posters and illustrations ever since. Newell's work has been featured in several music papers and magazines – notably the influential *Dazed and Confused* – and he produces all the artwork for the Everything on Toast record label.

Above left
Brudenell Social Club, Leeds
[Tom J. Newell],
November 2009

Above right
Hyde Park Picture House,
Leeds [Tom J. Newell],
May 2009

Right
Slow Club single launch party,
ICA, London [Tom J. Newell],
June 2009

POSTER BY MR. DREW MILLWARD - WWW.DREWMILLWARD.COM   WWW.SECRETSERPENTS.COM

Coventry-born Drew Millward began creating his abstract and often disturbing artworks in around 2005, designing posters for gigs that he and his friends put on. Since then, he has worked for bands including the Arctic Monkeys, the Melvins and Sonic Youth, and has had his work exhibited around the world. Millward does not create his artwork using digital technology, but instead draws the 'old-fashioned way', with pencils and pens. He even produces his own hand-made screen-prints.

Above left
Faith No More, Corn Exchange, Edinburgh [Drew Millward], August 2009

Above right
Black Moth Super Rainbow, Sticky Fingers, Little Rock, Arkansas [Drew Millward], June 2009

Below right
The Tallest Man On Earth, The Waiting Room, Omaha, Nebraska [Drew Millward], March 2009

Above right
Mogwai, The Slowdown,
Omaha, Nebraska
[Drew Millward],
May 2009

Below right
Big Business, *Mind the Drift*
tour [Drew Millward],
May 2009

CROSS-CURRENTS

America has its own rich tradition of rock poster design stretching back to the late 1960s, when psychedelic posters were created for the San Francisco ballroom scene. Today, a number of important American designers have produced some well-known posters for British bands and venues. Many of these artists (perhaps not surprisingly, given its place in the history of American rock art) are based on America's West Coast.

With a career as a graphic artist spanning 40 years, Dennis Loren has long been a catalyst for creative activity. Loren has managed to combine designing posters with supporting and mentoring other artists – including those whose work has crossed the Atlantic to the UK.

Born in Detroit, Michigan in 1946, Loren settled in the San Francisco Bay area in 1967 to design posters, including concert posters for Muddy Waters, Jimi Hendrix and the Velvet Underground. In the late seventies Loren moved back to Detroit, and in the late eighties he became a staff member on the magazine, *Creem*. In 2000, after 15 years in Los Angeles working for the music industry, Loren moved back to the San Francisco area to work with Gary Grimshaw, who is well known for his sixties Grande Ballroom posters and his illustration and layout work at *Creem*.

The phenomenon of artists based in America designing posters for the British rock scene has its roots in the nineties, at events like the annual poster exhibition at the Hall of Flowers in San Francisco's Golden Gate Park, the formation of the Rock Poster Society in 1999, and the American Poster Institute, founded by artist Frank Kozik. Kozik was also responsible for organizing the first Flatstock

Gig Poster Convention, which has become a key event in the US poster industry calendar. Today, Flatstock Conventions are held annually in Austin, Seattle, Chicago, San Francisco and Hamburg, Germany. The 1990s poster events sparked a revival of interest in rock posters, and consequently a renaissance in poster design – a by-product of which was the 'crossover' of American artists designing for UK events.

Loren explains: 'Frank Kozik should be lauded, because he long ago (after most venues in the USA stopped making posters) figured out that posters could sell at concerts to fans, just like T-shirts, CDs and other band merchandise. Frank's revolutionary thinking really reinvigorated the modern-day poster scene. He made deals with bands, venues and promoters, providing them with posters, if he was allowed to sell an agreed number of the copies of that poster to cover his printing costs and pay himself a wage.'

Loren's own experience was similar to that of other designers who, using what he calls the 'Kozik plan', have been commissioned to create posters for venues in the UK: 'I did the Shepherd's Bush White Stripes poster, using the Kozik plan. For many of the posters I did for the White Stripes (and other Detroit bands), I would be contacted by their booking agent in New York, because the bands would be on the road touring. They would tip me off on upcoming concerts and we would ship them to the venue. At one of the early Flatstock shows, I was approached by Richard Goodall, of the Richard Goodall Gallery in Manchester, England. He asked if I would be interested in doing some posters for the Rock City venue in Nottingham. He'd seen the work that I had done for the White Stripes and he liked my style. Richard was also having Emek, Justin Hampton

Above
Kings Of Leon, Rock City,
Nottingham [Guy Burwell],
December 2004

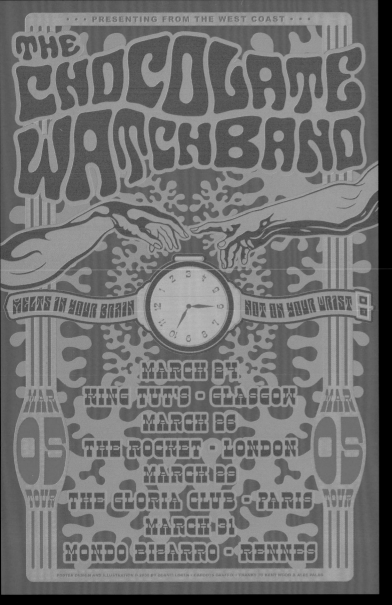

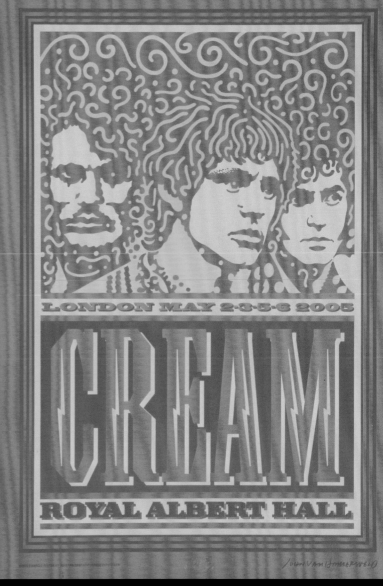

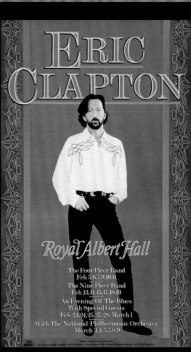

Above left
Chocolate Watchband Tour
poster [Dennis Loren],
March 2005

Above right
Cream, Royal Albert Hall,
London [John Van Hamersveld],
May 2005

Below left
Brian Wilson, Royal Albert Hall,
London [Mark London],
July 2005

Below centre
The Who, Wembley Arena,
London [Gary Grimshaw],
October 1989

Below right
Eric Clapton, Royal Albert Hall,
London [Gary Grimshaw],
February–March 1991

MONDAY SIXTH OF FEBRUARY 2006   BRIDGEWATER HALL MANCHESTER UK

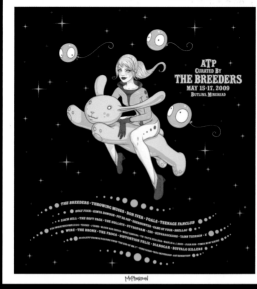

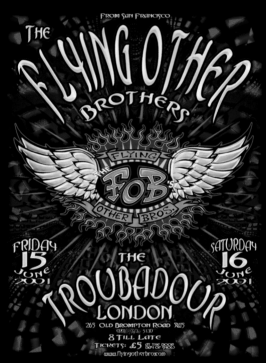

ermaine Rogers and some other American artists do osters for Rock City.'

Among the other artists whose work has crossed ver in this way is John Van Hamersveld, who created osters for various superstars in the 1960s and more ecently for Eric Clapton, Stevie Winwood and the 005 Cream reunion tour. Another important name is mek, part of a three-artist collective known as PNE Post Neo Explosionism), with fellow poster designers ustin Hampton and Jermaine Rogers. Key in this xport of US talent has been the Firehouse Kustom Rockart Company located near San Francisco in Oakland, run by two artists and master screen-printers, Chuck Sperry and Ron Donovan. Other ames Loren cites as worthy of mention are Tara McPherson, Guy Burwell (both of whom he met at the rst Flatstock Convention), Leia Bell, Chris Shaw, requent collaborator Mark London and his old friend

Gary Grimshaw, whose UK work preceded the 1990s poster relationship with the US, and included posters for the Who reunion at Wembley and an Eric Clapton show at the Royal Albert Hall.

There is a certain 'retro' feel to many of the artists designing for UK venues and bands, which Loren feels is to be expected: 'I'm an older guy, so that's my excuse, but many of the younger American artists are greatly influenced by the work of sixties artists, such as Wes Wilson, Stanley Mouse, Alton Kelley, Victor Moscoso – and especially the late and great Rick Griffin, who many of us cite as a major influence. One could say the same thing about Nashville's Hatch Show Print, established in 1875, and the much more recent work of Art Chantry, Frank Kozik and Emek. These last three artists have become very influential on yet another whole new generation of poster artists.'

Above left
Nick Cave, Bridgewater Hall,
Manchester [Emek],
February 2006

Above right
All Tomorrow's Parties Festival,
curated by the Breeders
[Tara McPherson],
May 2009

Below right
The Flying Other Brothers,
The Troubadour, London
[Chris Shaw],
June 2001

Opposite, above left
The Decemberists, Vicar Street,
Dublin [Leia Bell],
February 2007

Opposite, above right
Wolfmother, Hammersmith
Apollo, London
[Justin Hampton],
February 2007

Opposite, below left
The Coral, King's Parade,
Birkenhead
[Jermaine Rogers],
June 2003

Opposite, below right
Eric Clapton, Royal Albert Hall,
London [Chuck Sperry and
Ron Donovan/The Firehouse],
May 2009

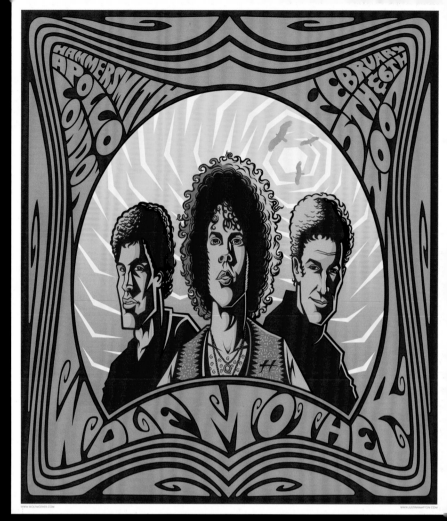

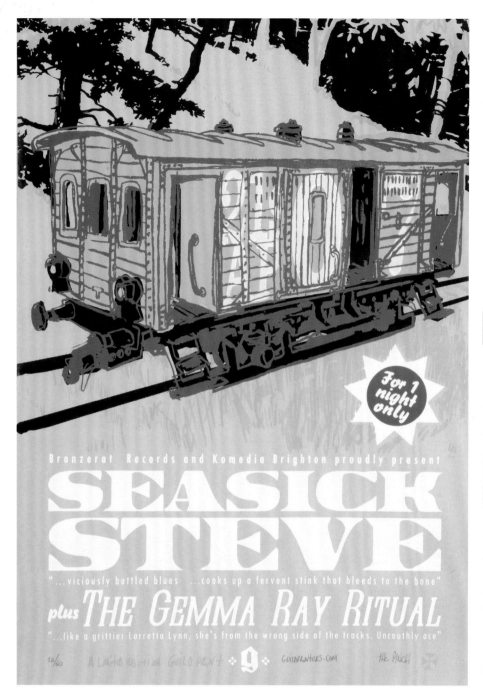

The designer known as The Pinch was first attracted to poster design in the mid-1990s, when he searched the internet for obscure bands he was keen to know more about. Ten years later, at the founding of the Brighton Rock Art Group (BRAG), he used its facilities to develop his print-making skills. 'It's great looking back on this early work because the gig poster is, and always will be, an inherently nostalgic art form, but I'm also keen to see what's coming next.' He describes his ambition in poster art as being, 'Fuelled by a desire to win a hallowed place for [his] work on the bedroom walls of college girls around the world.'

Above left
Seasick Steve, Komedia, Brighton [The Pinch], April 2007

Above right from top
Get Cape. Wear Cape. Fly, The Wedge [The Pinch], June 2008

Gringo Star UK tour flyer [The Pinch], 2008

The Dirt Bombs, University of London Union [The Pinch], June 2008

Evangelicals, University of London Union [The Pinch], June 2008

LOOSE MUSIC in association with NOT THE SAME OLD BLUES CRAP present

NASHVILLE BABYLON

PETE MOLINARI PLUS BAND
GAVIN GLASS & THE HOLY SHAKERS
MASTER OF CEREMONIES: RALPH MCLEAN, BBC
FRIDAY 26TH SEPTEMBER
BLACK BOX
HILL ST, CATHEDRAL QUARTER, BELFAST
DOORS 7PM STARTS 8PM £14
BOX OFFICE: 028 9024 6609
www.openhousefestival.com

Not The Same Old Blues Crap proudly presents
The 'After The Heart Attack' Tour
SEASICK STEVE
& The Level Devils

with **GAFFER HEXAM**

Tues 30th Nov 2004
+ DJ's Joe Cushley & 'Too Bad' Jim
The 12 Bar Club
22-23 Denmark Place Denmark Street London WC2H 8NL
Doors 7.30 'til late - Admission £6
www.NotTheSameOldBluesCrap.co.uk

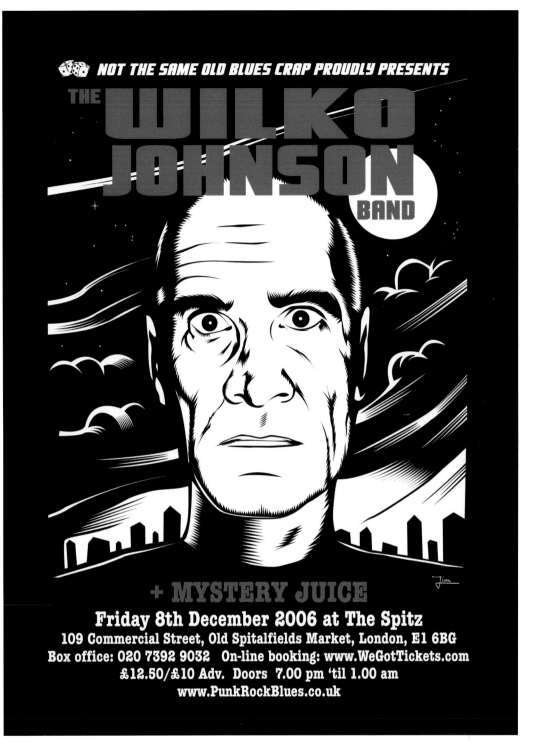

NOT THE SAME OLD BLUES CRAP PROUDLY PRESENTS

THE **WILKO JOHNSON** BAND

+ MYSTERY JUICE

Friday 8th December 2006 at The Spitz
109 Commercial Street, Old Spitalfields Market, London, E1 6BG
Box office: 020 7392 9032   On-line booking: www.WeGotTickets.com
£12.50/£10 Adv. Doors 7.00 pm 'til 1.00 am
www.PunkRockBlues.co.uk

Top left
Nashville Babylon, Belfast
[Too Bad Jim],
September 2008

Below left
Seasick Steve 'After the Attack'
tour poster [Too Bad Jim],
November 2004

Above right
Wilko Johnson, Spitz club,
London [Too Bad Jim],
December 2006

Too Bad Jim (a.k.a. Jim Johnstone), based in London, has created poster art for numerous rock 'n' roll and punk bands, blues artists and miscellaneous events. His most notable style is characterized by vintage, hot-rod-loving, burlesque-inspired designs. Solo exhibitions of his work have been held in London and Belfast.

Chris Hopewell began designing posters in the mid-1980s, and set up Bristol-based Jacknife Posters in 2006. Jacknife designer, Tape Ears (a.k.a Andy Ghosh), describes his influences as: 'The usual low-brow stuff – skateboard graphics, tattoo flash, punk zines, psychedelia, He-Man characters, Wilkinson's Halloween decorations, etc.' Tape Ears also admits to a lifelong obsession with ancient civilizations and mythology: 'Anything from Egyptian artifacts to Tibetan deities and Genghis Khan'.

Above left
Melt Banana, Thekla, Bristol
[Tape Ears],
June 2008

Above right
Queens of the Stone Age,
Apollo Hammersmith, London
[Chris Hopewell],
February 2008

Below right
Queens of the Stone Age, Rock
City, Nottingham
[Chris Hopewell],
November 2007

Amsterdam-born Sasha Morrison, who worked with Jacknife for two years, designed the Duke Spirit poster when the band asked designers from all over the UK to create a poster for each gig on the 2008 NME tour. Co-founder of Jacknife was Chris Hopewell's brother, known as Bear Hackenbush, who designed the poster shown on the right. Jacknife produces all of its posters on 320 gsm high-quality 'art'-style card, using Daler-Rowney System 3 acrylic paint. Each poster is numbered and signed as part of limited print run.

Above left
The Duke Spirit, NME Tour
[Sasha Morrison],
April 2008

Above right
Black Rebel Motorcycle Club,
Anson Rooms, Bristol
[Bear Hackenbush],
November 2007

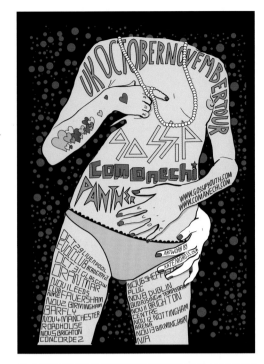

Kate Moross has created numerous designs for bands and clubs, as well as overseeing all projects within her ISO company (her work also appears in the previous chapter). Moross has worked for large companies, including Nike and Virgin, and runs her vinyl-only record label Isomorph Records. When creating artwork for a band, Moross says she looks to carve out a new aesthetic for every project: 'I try not to be influenced too much by current trends, but I like to have a lot of dialogue with the band and establish what they want as well as what I think they need.'

Above left
Gossip, UK Tour poster
[Kate Moross],
October 2006

Below left
New Young Pony Club, Scala
flyer [Kate Moross],
November 2006

Above right
Mystery Jets Acoustic Tour
[Kate Moross],
October 2006

Commercial artist Michael Cowell, based in Nottingham, works in paint, print, photography and digital media. Drawing inspiration from 'left-of-centre' sources, he designs album artwork for numerous bands. He also specializes in limited-edition, hand-painted gig posters. The Rolo Tomassi tour poster (below right) is based on a hand-drawn sketch. After adding further elements, including a 15th-century star map, to the original composition on a computer, Cowell burned screens during the print process to create rich layers of colour.

Above left
Loud Howls festival, The Gaff, London [Michael Cowell], April 2010

Above right
Monster Magnet, La Loco, Paris [Michael Cowell], December 2008

Below right
Rolo Tomassi tour poster [Michael Cowell], January 2009

Another member of the Brighton-based BRAG poster design collective, Jemma Treweek is an illustrator and printmaker who, in her own words, 'loves making posters, drinking tea, drawing and loud music'. Treweek screen-prints most of her work, which is then digitally tweaked. She has produced artwork for the band Bonde do Rolê, and artists Vashti Bunyan and Nina Nastasia, among others. Treweek's work, which is influenced by folk art, mermaids, dolls and Hans Holbein, has appeared in *The Guardian*, *Vogue*, *Mixmag* and several Japanese magazines.

Above left
Vashti Bunyan, Theatre Royal, Brighton [Jemma Treweek], May 2008

Below left
Kylesa, Szene, Vienna [Jemma Treweek], February 2008

Above right
Bonde do Rolê, Concorde 2, Brighton [Jemma Treweek], November 2007

Raised in Yorkshire, Kathryn Cooper graduated in fine art from Nottingham Trent University in 2002. After living in London for a period, she relocated to the edge of Ilkley Moor in Yorkshire. She channels her various designs and what she describes as 'self-publishing efforts' through her company and website, Cooper's Market. Cooper has collaborated in community projects, including a book about female asylum seekers in the UK. She also plays in a band called the Ice Cream Headaches.

Top left
Cowtown, Edin's
[Kathryn Cooper],
July 2008

Top centre
Zun Zun Egui, Brudenell Social
Club, Leeds [Kathryn Cooper],
July 2009

Top right
A Hawk and a Hacksaw,
Barden's Boudoir, London
[Kathryn Cooper],
June 2005

Above
Le Singe Blanc, Fenton,
Leeds [Kathryn Cooper],
June 2009

INDEX

CREDITS

Every effort has been made to trace and contact copyright holders. The publishers invite readers to notify them of any errors or omissions.

Copyright holder and artist

pp.16 (TL) and 17 (TL): Tony Booth; p.18: TL, Colin Duffield, R, Tony Booth; p.19: TR, Colin Duffield; p.22: TL, Colin Duffield; p.31: TR, Tony Booth; p.32: Courtesy of Hayward Archive (www.rockmusicprints.com); p.35: Brian Pike; p.36: © Peter Blake. All rights reserved, DACS 2010.; p.37: © Jasper Johns / VAGA, New York / DACS, London 2010.; p.45: Michael English, © Nigel Waymouth; p.49: TL, © Apple Corps Ltd., TR, Bob Dylan poster (1966) by Marijke Koger-Dunham of The Fool, (www.maryke.com); pp.50–57: All works by Hapshash and the Coloured Coat, © Nigel Waymouth; p.58–59: Original illustrations by Alan Aldridge from The Beatles Illustrated Lyrics 1969; p.61–62: TL, All works by Martin Sharp; pp.64–68: All works by Martin Sharp; p.69: TL, Martin Sharp, TR, Mike McInnerney (www.mikemcinnerney.com); p.70: TL, Nigel Waymouth, TR, Mike McInnerney (www.mikemcinnerney.com); p.71: TL, Janet Williamson, TR, Greg Irons; p.72: L, ©Subafilms Ltd.; p.73: TL, Dave Roe, TR, Jamie McGregor; p.77: TL, Image from King Crimson archive courtesy of DGM Ltd., (c) Robert Fripp, www.dgmlive.com for further info., TR, Haig Adishian; p.78, 79 (TR) and 80–81: All images © Copyright 2010 - Paul Whitehead, All rights reserved; p.83–85: Hipgnosis; p.86: TL, Hugh Gilmour; p.87: TL, Created by Steve Harradine, Copyright © Steve Harradine, All rights reserved. (www.steveharradine.com / harradineart@gmail.com); pp.89–93: Roger Dean; pp.94–95: Barney Bubbles; p.96: TL, George Underwood, TR, Photo by Duffy courtesy of Duffy Archive / (www.duffyphotographer.com); p.98: Photo by Clive Arrowsmith/Celebrity Pictures; p.99: TL, Artist, Geoff Halpin, © A&M Records, TR and BR, Nick de Ville and Brian Ferry; p.103: TR, Michael Beal; p.104: T and BR, Barry Jones; p.106: TL, Photo by Kate Simon, TR Photo by Caroline Coon; p.107: TL, Artwork by Ray Lowry, Photo by Pennie Smith; p.108: Poly Styrene; p.109: TR, Photo by Terry O'Neill; p.110: Designed by Malcolm Garrett, Artwork by Linder Sterling; p.111: TL, Malcolm Garrett, TR, Designed by Malcolm Garrett, Artwork by Linder Sterling; pp.112–114: Jamie Reid; p.118: TL, Artwork by Bill Smith, Photo by Martyn Goddard; p.119: Kavanagh; p.120: TR, Chris Morton,

TL and BR, Photo by Chris Gabrin; p.121: TL and BR, Designed by Barney Bubbles, photo by Chris Gabrin, TR, Keith Morris; p.123–127: Barney Bubbles; p.126: TL, Designed by Barney Bubbles, photo by Chris Gabrin; p.128: TR, Richard Butler; p.129: TL, Ian Wright; p.134: TR and TL, © John Pasche, BR, By permission of Freddy Bannister, Designed by Walker-Parkinson Design; pp.135–136: Martine Grainey (http://martinegrainey.com); p.137: TL, Artwork by David King, © Track Records, TR and R, Richard Evans; pp.139–141: Hugh Gilmour; p.140: TR, Hugh Gilmour and Joe Petagno; p.141: R, Hugh Gilmour and Shepard Fairey; p.142: TL, Peter Barrett and Andrew Biscomb, TR, Francis Drake and Fraser Gray; p.143: TL and TR, Stylorouge, CR, Keith Breeden at Design KB, © Universal Records; p.145: Assorted Images; p.146: TL, Morrissey (photo of Shelagh Delaney artwork), TC, Morrissey (photo by James R. Reid), TR, Morrissey (photo by Jürgen Vollmer); p.147: Microdot; p.148: TL and BL, Logo by Designers Republic © Island Records, TR, Stylorouge; p.149: TL and TR, Artwork by Banksy, BR, © Julian Opie / (www.julianopie.com); p.151–153: Vaughan Oliver; p.157: © Central Station Design; p.158: Trevor Jackson at Trevor Jackson Design / (www.trevor-jackson.com); p.159: TL, Design by Me Company, Art Direction by Paul White, Logo Design by Jill Mumford, TR, Design by Me Company, Art Direction by Paul White; pp.160–163: © Peter Saville; p.164: TC and TR, Steven Perry (Pez), BL, Me; p.165: TL, Rachel Goldstein and Ben Pearson, BR, Ria Dastidar; p.166: Design and Illustration Daniel Koch @ Zip Design; p.167: LC and TL, Ali Augur (www.aliaugur.com), TR, Russell Reid @ Russtle (www.russtle.com); p.168: TR, Kate Moross / (www.katemoross.com) and Jack Featherstone; pp.168–169: Kate Moross / (www.katemoross.com); pp.170–171: iwant Design; pp.172–173: Non-format; p.174: Non-format and Jake Walters; p.175: Design by bleach (www.wearebleach.co.uk) / Illustration: Hello Marine, Alex Chappell and Si Scott; p.179: TL, Stanley Donwood, BR, La Boca; pp.180–182: All images, Massive Attack campaign posters 1998-1999, Art Direction and Design by Tom Hingston Studio and Robert Del Naja, Photography by Nick Knight; p.183: Art Direction and Design by Vaughan Oliver, Photo by Simon Larbalestier; p.185: TL, Dave Roe, TR, Design by Tim Biskup © All Tomorrow's Parties, FR, Design by bleach, Illustration by Steve Wilson; p.186: TL and BL, Art Direction by Cally

(www.antar.cc), TR, Paul Thompson; p.187: Jamie Hewlett; p.188: Matt Ferres / (www.ferres.co.uk); p.189: Stylorouge; p.190: Pete Murgatroyd / (www.petemurgatroyd.co.uk); p.191: Tom J. Newell / (www.tomjnewell.com); pp.192–193: Drew Millward; p.194: GUYBURWELL / (guyburwell.com); p.195: TL, Dennis Loren (www.dennisloren.com / dennisloren@gmail.com), TR, John Van Hamersveld, RC and FR, Gary Grimshaw, R, Mark London; p.196: TL, EMEK / EMEK Studios, Inc. / emek@emek.net / (www.emek.net), TR, Tara McPherson / (www.taramcpherson.com), TC, Chris Shaw; p.197: TL: Leia Bell / (www.leiabell.com), TR, Justin Hampton (www.justinhampton.com), BL, Jermaine Rogers / (JermaineRogers.com), BR, Chuck Sperry and Ron Donovan, Firehouse Kustom Rockart Company; p.198: The Pinch; p.199: Jim Johnstone / (www.toobadjim.co.uk); p.200: TL, Tape Ears (Andy Ghosh), TR and TC, Chris Hopewell, Designer at Jacknife; p.201: TL, Sasha Morrison at Jacknife / (sashamorrison@gmail.com / www.jacknifeposters.com), TR, Bear Hackenbush Designer at Jacknife; p.202: Kate Moross / (www.katemoross.com); p.203: Michael Cowell / (www.michael-cowell.com); p.204: Jemma Treweek / (www.jemmatreweek.co.uk); p.205: Kathryn Cooper / (www.coopersmarket.com)

Poster suppliers

Mark Adams, p.96: TL; Jenny Ross of Adelita Ltd., pp.94–95: all, p.121: TL, p.123: TL, TR, p.124, p.125: TL, TR; Allposters.co.uk, p.49: TR, p.72: BL, p.84: T, p.85: TL, TR, p.187; All Tomorrow's Parties, p.185: TR; Amazon.co.uk, p.97, p.186: TR; Clive Arrowsmith / Celebrity Pictures, p.98; Ali Augur, p.167: TL, BL; Beatleshop.co.uk, p.18: TR; bleach, p.175, p.185: BR; Bill Bruford, p.77: TR, p.87: TR; Buddyhollymemorabilia.com, p.15: TR; Cally at www.antar.cc, p.186: TL, BL; Central Station Design, p.157; Kathryn Cooper, p.205; Corbis, p.37; Glenn Cornick, p.79: TL, BL; Michael Cowell, p.203; Roger Crimlis, p.35, p.106: TL, p.108, p.109: TR, p.110, p.119, p.121: TR, p.123: BR, p.127, p.128: TR, p.129: TR; Cypher Arts and Galleries, p.78, p.79: TR, p.80–81; Ria Dastidar, p.165: BR; Roger Dean, p.89, p.90: TR, p.91–93: all; King Crimson archive courtesy of DGM Ltd., p.77; Discogs.com, p.142: BR, p.145: T; Endclub.co.uk, p.165: TR; Mike Evans, p.104: T, BR, p.145: BL, p.185: TL, BL; Richard Evans / (www.rdevans.com), p.21: TR, p.35: TL,

p.137: TR, BR; Exetermemories.co.uk, p.16: TR, p.33: TR, p.40: TL; Matthew Ferres, p.188; Gemm.com, p.142: TR; Hugh Gilmour, p.86: TL, p.139–141: all; Peter Golding, p.15: TL, p.18: TL, p.19: TR, p.21: TL, p.22: TL, p.59, pp.61–63, p.69: TR, p.70–71, p.133; Martine Grainey, pp.135–136; Steve Harradine, p.87: TL; Hayward Archive / (www.rockmusicprints.com), p.19: TL, p.32; Martin Hendry of M&N Publishing, pp.44–45, p.49: TL, pp.50–58, pp.64–68, p.69: TL, p.73: TR; iwant Design, pp.170–171; Jacknife, pp.200–201; Trevor Jackson, p.158; The Knebworth House, p.134: BR; Dennis Loren: pp.194–197; Gary Loveridge, p.96: TR, p.103: TR, p.105, p.106: TR, p.107, p.109: TL, p.112–118, p.120, p.121: TR, p.125: BL, BR, p.126, p.128: TL, pp.150–151, p.152: TL, BL, p.153; Manchester District Music Archive, p.111: TR; Maximumrnb.com, p.16: TL, p.17: TR, TL, p.19: BL, p.23: TR, p.24, p.25, pp.26–27, p.31, p.33: TL, p.34, pp.38–39, p.40: TL, pp.41–43, p.60, p.103: TL; Jamie McGregor, p.73: TL; Drew Millward, pp.192–193; Kate Moross, pp.168–169, p.202; Moviegoods.com, p.72: T; Peter Murgatroyd, p.190; Muse.mu, p.179: BR; Nearfest.com, p.90: TL; Tom Newell, p.191; Non-format, pp.172–174; Vaughan Oliver, pp.147–149, p.183; Tony Ortiz, p.86: TR; Big O book (Osiris Publishing), p.99: TR, TL, p.137 TL; Danny Parnes, p.22: TR, p.23: TL; John Pasche, p.134: TL, TR; Ben Pearson, p.165: TL; Steven Perry (Pez), p.164, TC, TR; Phatmedia.co.uk, p.164: BL; The Pinch, p.198: all; Popartuk.com, p.83, p.179: TL, TR; Pushposters.co.uk, p.36, p.143: TL; Russell Reid, p.167: TR; Courtesy of www.retro-madness.co.uk, p.129: TL; Peter Saville, pp.160–163; Stylorouge, p.143: TR, p.152: TR, p.189; Teeshirtsrock.com, p.99: BR; Storm Thorgerson, p.84, BL, BR, p.85: BR; Tom Hingston Studio, pp.180–182; Too Bad Jim, p.199; Jemma Treweek, p.204; Vtmusic.co.uk, p.143: CR; Andy Wake, p.111: TR; Wikipedia.org, p.145: BR; Wolfgang's Vault, p.142: TL; Zip Design, p.166

T   – Top
TL   – Top left
TR   – Top right
TC   – Top centre
BL   – Below left
BR   – Below right
LC   – Left centre
FR   – Far right
R   – Right
RC   – Right centre

AUTHOR BIOGRAPHIES & ACKNOWLEDGEMENTS

Mike Evans

With a background as a musician on the sixties rock scene, Mike Evans began writing about popular music in the seventies. As a freelance journalist he was a regular contributor to *Melody Maker* and his work appeared in UK rock magazines, including *Sounds* and *Cream*. As author his books have included the much-acclaimed *The Art of the Beatles* in 1984, the best-selling *Elvis: A Celebration* (2002), *Waking Up In New York City* in 2003, and *Ray Charles: The Birth of Soul* in 2005. *The Beats* (an illustrated account of the Beat Generation) appeared in 2007, and *Woodstock: Three Days That Shook the World* in 2009. He lives and works in London, dividing his time between writing and a freelance editorial consultancy.

Paul Palmer-Edwards

From his earliest employment, Paul Palmer-Edwards has been fortunate enough to combine his love of music with a love of design – whether it was making coffee for Brian Eno (once!), or pasting up music ads and record covers for EMI Records in the seventies, he still managed to find time to perform with a succession of bands (appearing on the short-lived *Cabaret Futura* live album). Throughout the eighties, he honed his design skills, working for many of the major design companies of that era, while continuing to gig around London, until finally hanging up his guitar to concentrate on design full time. In 2000, he co-founded Grade Design, a design studio specializing in publishing, and has since worked on many award-winning projects as well as being a regular contributor to the *Mojo* letters page.

Authors' Acknowledgements

Many thanks to Roger Crimlis, Roger Dean, Richard Evans, Malcolm Garrett, Hugh Gilmour, John Gilsenan, Peter Golding, Paul Gorman, Mark Hayward, Martin Hendry, Chris Hopewell, Marijke Koger, Dennis Loren, Gary Loveridge, Barry Miles, Non-Format Design, Vaughan Oliver, John Pasche, Steve Perry (Pez), Jenny Ross, Peter Saville, Stylorouge.

Editors' Acknowledgements

This book would not have been possible without the assistance of a variety of people, many of whom gave items from their collections, along with their valuable help and advice, in a spirit of pure generosity: Mark Adams, James Anderson, Ali Augur, Ian Ball (Albinal), Richard Barnes, Dave Bedford and www.liddypool.com, Tony Booth, Bill Bruford, Cally, Henry Cobbold at Knebworth House, John Cooper of Cerysmatic Factory, Glenn Cornick, Michael Cowell, Martin Creasey, Roger Crimlis, Ria Dastidar, Albie Donnelly, Colin Duffield, Chris Duffy, Nicky Ellis, Matt Ferres, Michelle Franco, William Frank at Xylo Design, Richard Goodall of the Richard Goodall Gallery (www.richardgoodallgallery.com), Martine Grainey, Stephan Heimbecher, Nicola Joss, Elizabeth Kerr at CameraPress, Sam Leach, Dennis Loren, Gary Loveridge, Dave Manvell, Ian Maxwell (www.rocknrollbritain.com), Pippa Mole, Kate Moross, Roger Multon, Hugh O'Donnell, Mary Patel at Zip Design, Ben Pearson, Marc Picken, Paul Trynka, Russell Reid, Dr Paul Rennie, Doug Smith, Jeff Strawman, Sue at Ombfc, Alwyn Turner, Nik Turner, Steve Turner, George Underwood, David Walker, Tobias Warwick Jones, Amy Waskett at Tom Hingston Studios, Chris Welch, Colin Welch, Paul Whitehead and Dan Shapiro of Cypher Arts, Arlene Wszalek.